AIKIDO

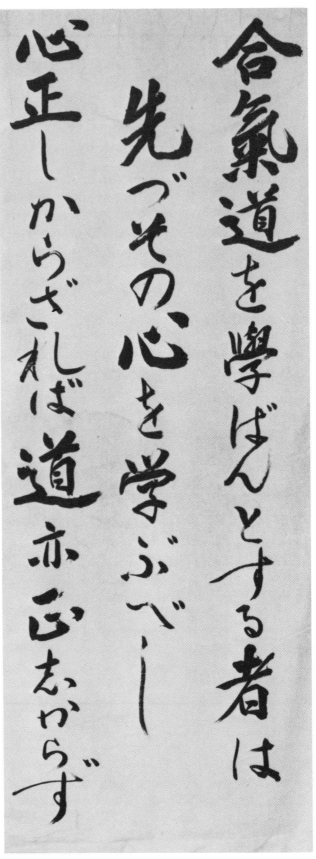

合氣道を學ばんとする者は
先づその心を學ぶべし
心正しからざれば道亦正しからず

Calligraphy and verse by Shirata Rinjiro.
Translation on title page.

AIKIDO

The Way
of Harmony

By John Stevens

Under the direction
of Shirata Rinjiro

Those who wish to learn Aikido
Must first study its spirit;
If one's heart is not true
The Way will never be attained.

SHAMBHALA

BOSTON & LONDON 1985

SHAMBHALA PUBLICATIONS, INC.
Horticultural Hall
300 Massachusetts Avenue
Boston, Massachusetts 02115

9   8   7   6
Distributed in the United States by Random House and in
Canada by Random House of Canada, Ltd.
Printed in the United States of America.

Library of Congress Cataloging in Publication Data
Stevens, John, 1947–
    Aikido, the way of harmony.
    1. Aikido. I. Shirata, Rinjiro. II. Title.
GV1114.35.S76   1983   613.7'1   82-42680
ISBN 0-87773-229-9 (pbk.)
ISBN 0-394-71426-1 (Random House: pbk.)

Text design by Lee Graphics, Boulder CO
Cover design by Julia Runk
Typography by The Art Workers, Boulder, CO
Printed and bound by McNaughton & Gunn, Saline MI

Contents

Foreword   vii

Acknowledgments   ix

INTRODUCTION   1

  1 The Founder, Ueshiba Morihei   3

  2 Fifty Years of Aikido   15

  3 The Heart of Aikido   21

  4 Aikido Training   25

AIKIDO TECHNIQUES

  5 Kokyu-ho: Breath-Meditation   29

  6 Kamae: Stance   53

  7 Shiho-nage: Four Directions Throw   61

  8 Irimi-nage: Entering Throw   89

  9 Kaiten: Open and Turn   103

 10 Kokyu-ho Waza: Breath-Power Techniques   127

 11 Taninsu-gake: Multiple Attack   137

 12 Osae Waza: Pinning Techniques   153

 13 Ushiro Waza: Rear Techniques   177

Glossary of Japanese Terms   195

Hanzawa Yoshimi Sensei.

Foreword

I am extremely gratified by the publication of *Aikido: The Way of Harmony*, which is a most valuable contribution to the advancement of Aikido throughout the world. The book is the result of many years of diligent research. For more than a decade, John Stevens has been studying in Japan, attaining extensive theoretical and practical knowledge of Buddhism, art, literature, and other aspects of Oriental culture. He also has a wide acquaintance with various martial arts, concentrating on Aikido as his "Way of Harmony" first as a trainee in my *dojo* in Sendai and now as an instructor at Tohoku College of Social Welfare. Working closely with Shirata Sensei he has produced a comprehensive guide to the essential inner and outer factors of Aikido.

On a lower level, the path of Aiki enables us to harmonize the three functions of body, mind, and *kokyu* and then to blend our movements with those of our partner; on a higher level, it is a Way to become one with nature, to function in harmony with the universe. Thus Aikido transcends the boundaries of time and space, working to unite all people—human beings who share the same joys and sorrows, the same dreams and disappointments—of East and West in one family. If there is one creed that is needed in today's society, it is a "Way of Harmony" that can reconcile opposition and antagonism.

With this in mind, I encourage all Aikido practitioners to apply the principles set forth in the following pages in daily life as well as in the training hall.

Hanzawa Yoshimi, Roku-dan
Director, Tohoku Aikido Association

*For my teachers, fellow practitioners,
and students in Sendai*

Acknowledgments

Japanese names are given in the native manner, i.e., family name first. "Founder" is the English equivalent of *kaiso*, an expression commonly used when referring to Ueshiba Morihei. "Sensei" is the title used for respected teachers.

The biography of the Founder is based on two recently published books, *Ueshiba Morihei Den* ("Biography of Ueshiba Morihei") by Ueshiba Kisshomaru and *Bu no Shinjin* ("True Man of Bu") by Sunadomari Kamanori, plus Daito-ryu accounts and Shirata Sensei's personal recollections.

Like any true master, Shirata Sensei refuses to "pose" or be photographed in an unnatural studio environment. The photo sequences were shot in the Yamagata City Budokan under normal practice conditions. The scroll in the center reads "Aikido" and the one on the left says, "The Way of the Gods and the Way of Bu are originally not two different paths" *(Shin bu genrai muni do)*.

I am most grateful to Hanzawa Yoshimi Sensei for providing a foreword and his kind instruction over the years. I deeply appreciate the great encouragement and unstinting assistance of the instructors and practitioners of the Sendai Aikido Association and the cooperation of my students in the Tohoku College of Social Welfare Aikido Club. Doshu Ueshiba Kisshomaru and Saito Morihiro Sensei graciously supplied photographs of the Founder. The staff at Shambhala Publications deserve the highest praise, especially Sam Bercholz and Larry Mermelstein—an author could not hope for a finer publisher and editor. The debt owed Shirata Sensei for inspiration and guidance can never be adequately repaid.

John Stevens
Sendai, 1983

INTRODUCTION

1

The Founder,
Ueshiba Morihei

Ueshiba Morihei, the founder of Aikido, was born on December 14,* 1883, to a farm family in an area of Wakayama Prefecture now known as Tanabe. He was the fourth born, and only son, among five children. From his solidly built father Yoroku, Morihei inherited a samurai's determination and interest in public affairs, and from his mother Yuki, he inherited an intense interest in religion, poetry, and art.

The boy at first was rather weak and sickly, preferring to read books indoors than play outside. Around the age of eight, Morihei began learning the Chinese classics under the direction of a Shingon priest, but was more fascinated by esoteric Buddhist rites, especially the *homa* fire service. He loved to listen to the miraculous legends associated with the wonder-working saints En no Gyoja and Kobo Daishi, who spent part of their lives in the sacred Kumano district not far from Morihei's home. Morihei even thought of becoming a Buddhist priest himself someday.

As an antidote to his son's daydreaming and high-strung behavior, Yoroku recounted the exploits of Morihei's famous great-grandfather Kichiemon, said to be one of the strongest samurai of the day, and encouraged the boy to take up *sumo* wrestling and swimming. Morihei gradually became stronger, and realized the necessity of possessing adequate power after his father was attacked one night by a gang of thugs hired by a rival politician.

Morihei left middle school after a year—the classes bored him and his nervous energy demanded a more practical outlet. Always good at mathematics, Morihei enrolled in a *soroban* (abacus) academy; less than twelve

*November 16 according to the old lunar calendar.

months later he was acting as an assistant instructor. Still in his teens, Morihei took a job as an assessor in the local tax office. He was an excellent worker, but during the course of his duties he was obliged to administer a new tax law directed at farmers and fishermen. Convinced that the regulations were grossly unfair, he resigned in righteous indignation and became a leader of the protest movement, much to the chagrin of his councilman father. Yoroku gave him a substantial sum of money, saying, "Take this and try to find something you would really like to do."

Hoping to become a great merchant, Morihei went to Tokyo in 1901. He managed to open a small stationery supply store, but commerce suited him no better than tax accounting, and he closed down the business in a few months. During his brief stay in Tokyo, Morihei did discover that he had a definite affinity for martial arts, greatly enjoying his study of jujutsu at the Kito-ryu dojo and swordsmanship at the Shinkage-ryu training center. A severe case of beri-beri caused him to return home. Shortly thereafter, at the age of nineteen, he married Itogawa Hatsu.

Morihei quickly regained his health, but was at a loss what to do next. Storm clouds were brewing between Russia and Japan so the impetuous young man decided to enlist in the army and seek some adventure. Unfortunately, Morihei, who stood just over five feet tall, was slightly under the minimum height requirement. Extremely upset, he spent the next several months training alone in the mountains, hanging from branches with weights on his legs and performing other stretching exercises to extend his spine the necessary half-inch.

Morihei passed the physical on his next attempt and in 1903 joined the infantry. The tireless energy of the fastidious soldier caught the attention of his superiors and he was rapidly promoted. Morihei earned a reputation for his zeal for hard training and his unusual skill at bayonet fighting. He served with distinction in Manchuria during the Russo-Japanese War of 1904-5, displaying for the first time his uncanny ability to anticipate an attack—he said that he could sense when a bullet was coming his way even before it was fired—and his commanding officer wanted to

recommend him for admission to the National Military Academy. For various reasons, Morihei declined the position and resigned from active duty. During his four years in the military, Morihei greatly improved his physical condition, building himself up to a rock-hard one hundred eighty pounds, and earned his first menkyo, teaching license, for a martial art from Nakai Masakatsu of the Yagyu-ryu. (The dojo was located in Sakai, a suburb of Osaka where Morihei was stationed.)

Morihei returned to the farm and married life, but remained restless. Hot-tempered and irritable, almost manic-depressive, he began to act strangely—locking himself in his room for hours to pray, jumping up in the middle of the night to douse himself with cold water, fasting in the mountains for days on end. Concerned with his son's erratic behavior, Yoroku built a dojo on the property and invited the well-known jujutsu teacher Takaki Kiyoichi to teach there. Morihei threw himself into the training and his disposition improved considerably.

During this period, Morihei came under the influence of the noted scholar Minakata Kumagusu (who, incidentally, had spent many years studying in the United States and England). Kumagusu vigorously opposed the government's plan to consolidate smaller Shinto shrines under the jurisdiction of larger ones, primarily because he felt the sentiments of the local residents would be ignored. Morihei supported Kumagusu's position, actively petitioning officials, writing protest letters to newspapers, organizing demonstrations, and so on. Morihei's involvement in this affair increased his interest in national politics; when the government called for volunteers to settle in the underdeveloped land of Hokkaido, Kumagusu encouraged him to consider the possibility, especially in light of Japan's future food needs. The pioneer spirit of "creating something out of nothing" appealed to Morihei; in addition, the village now had many unemployed farmers and fishermen. A town meeting was held and more than eighty people agreed to emigrate en masse. In the spring of 1912, the twenty-nine-year-old Morihei, with his wife and their two-year-old daughter, led the group to the wilderness of Hokkaido.

The group settled in the frigid northeast section of the island around the village of

Shirataki. Things began inauspiciously—no one knew how to grow potatoes, and early frosts, cool summers, and harsh winters wiped out the other crops three years in a row. Having to subsist on wild vegetables and fish, not a few of the pioneers regretted their move, and did not hesitate to blame Morihei for their plight. Luckily, circumstances improved as the demand for lumber soared and the village prospered. A fire that destroyed the central district was a severe blow, but due largely to Morihei's ceaseless efforts, everything was rebuilt within a year. He was elected to the village council and was respectfully known as the "King of Shirataki."

The tremendous muscular strength of Morihei's arms was said to be a result of the years of heavy logging in Shirataki; everyday he wrestled with huge 100 to 200 pound pieces of lumber. A number of anecdotes survive from this Shirataki period: once he single-handedly lifted a horse and wagon from a deep ditch; he subdued three bandits who tried to rob him; he calmed a marauding bear and shared his lunch with it. The most significant event of his stay in Hokkaido was his meeting with Takeda Sokaku, grandmaster of Daito-ryu Aiki-jutsu.

By tradition, the Daito-ryu was founded c. 1100 A.D. by Minamoto (Genji) Yoshimitsu, sixth generation descendant of the Emperor Seiwa. Yoshimitsu's son Yoshikiyo moved to Koga (present-day Yamanashi Prefecture) and established the Takeda clan; the art was secretly transmitted among family members from generation to generation. In 1574, Takeda Kunitsugu moved to Aizu (Fukushima Prefecture) where the special "oshiki-uchi" (also known as o-dome) techniques were taught exclusively to high ranking samurai of the Aizu-han for the next three hundred years.

Actually, the origin of the Daito-ryu seems less ancient and more prosaic. Takeda Soemon (1758-1853) taught a system known as aiki-in-yo-ho, "the aiki system of yin and yang," which he passed on to Saigo Tanomo, chief retainer of the Aizu lord. Saigo also had training in Misoguchi-ryu swordsmanship and Koshu-ryu military science. The Aizu samurai were die-hard supporters of the old military regime and fiercely resisted the new Meiji government, being among the last to capitulate in 1868. Certain that Tanomo had been killed in the final battle with the Imperial Forces and determined to preserve the honor of the Saigo name, his mother, his wife, his five daughters, and fourteen other members of his family committed ritual suicide. Tanomo's life had been spared, however; following this tragedy, he served as a Shinto priest in various districts and adopted Shida Shiro as his disciple-son. The extremely talented Shiro mastered the oshiki-uchi techniques, later applying them with great effect as the star of Kano Jigoro's newly founded Kokodan school of Judo. At an open tournament in 1889, assistant instructor Shiro defeated all comers with his yama-arashi ("mountain-storm") oshiki-uchi technique, thus securing the reputation of the Kokodan. (Shiro's story has been fictionalized in the popular Sugata Sanshiro series of novels and movies.) Not much later, however, Shiro—probably torn between his debt to his adoptive father Tanomo and his respect for Jigoro—abandoned the practice of both systems, moved to Nagasaki, and devoted himself to classical archery (kyudo) the rest of his life.

Fortunately, the aging Tanomo had another worthy heir: Takeda Sokaku (1860-1943), Soemon's grandson. (Since Sokaku's father Sokichi concentrated on sumo wrestling rather than aiki-in-yo-ho, the family tradition temporarily passed to an "outsider.")

Sokaku was no beginner; at an early age he had obtained teaching licenses in Ono-ha Itto-ryu swordsmanship and Hozoin spear-fighting as well as studying with the "swordsman-saint" Sakakibara Kenkichi of the Jikishin-kage-ryu. A demon swordsman, Sokaku "stormed" dojos all over the country, engaging in thousands of contests. He almost never lost. He reportedly had more than one battle with a live sword; once he got involved in a fight with a group of construction workers and killed seven or eight of them.*

* Details of this semilegendary tale have been embellished over the years—one version has Sokaku fighting off three hundred enraged workers armed with iron rods, fire axes, and stones in the heart of Tokyo, with twelve slain and many more wounded. It appears that the incident occurred in Fukushima and that Sokaku cut his way through a crowd of fifty or so workers and escaped rather than standing his ground, meeting wave after wave of attackers.

When Tanomo transmitted the last of his knowledge to Sokaku in 1898, he told him, "The way of the sword is over; from now on make these marvelous techniques known everywhere." Sokaku modified the *oshiki-uchi* techniques based on his long years of practical experience; he designated his composite system "Daito-ryu Aiki-jutsu," and should rightly be considered its founder.

Now an invincible master of Aiki, Sokaku traveled widely, attracting a large number of disciples; he was reputed to have had around thirty thousand disciples and nearly every *budoka* of note in that era was his student in one way or the other. One of them was a Westerner, an American named Charles Perry.

In 1903, Perry, an English instructor at a secondary school in Sendai, was riding a train and asked the conductor to check the first-class ticket of the shabbily dressed Japanese man down the aisle. When Sokaku demanded to know why only he was requested to show his ticket, the conductor told him the American gentleman didn't think he belonged in this car. The short-tempered Sokaku jumped to his feet and went over to Perry for an explanation. Perry stood up, brandishing both fists, sure that his six-foot height would intimidate the diminutive Sokaku. Sokaku grabbed both of Perry's wrists and applied what modern Aikido students know as "*yonkyo*"; the pain brought Perry to his knees and then Sokaku threw him toward the end of the car. After making a humble apology, Perry asked permission to learn something of the art himself. The story goes that Perry later reported this encounter and details of his studies with Sokaku to the State Department in Washington; Teddy Roosevelt heard about it and asked that someone be sent to teach in the United States. Harada Shinzo of Sendai was dispatched to the U.S. for some months and it may well be that an American president was himself introduced to the mysteries of Aiki before Ueshiba Morihei.

Sokaku never had a permanent *dojo* of his own, preferring to attract disciples by Perry-like chance encounters, challenges to local *kendo* and *judo* instructors—the loser became the victor's pupil—and formal demonstrations. Sokaku would hold a twisted piece of paper and ask a volunteer to take one end; suddenly the person at the other end would start to rise off the floor. Then Sokaku would have his hands firmly tied behind his back and invite the participants to try and throw or pin him; regardless of what they attempted or from what direction they came, they could not get him down; on the contrary, each one hit the floor himself. For a finale, he would ask all those present to grab him at once; in a flash everyone would be sent flying. Another favorite trick of his was to be lifted on the shoulders of the five or six biggest onlookers; Sokaku somehow made them collapse in a heap with him on top and they would remain there immovable until he let them up. Needless to say, many eagerly became students after such an impressive performance.

Morihei was first introduced to Sokaku in 1915 at an inn in Engaru. Although Morihei was a pretty tough fellow himself—on occasion he was mistaken for Sokaku because they were about the same size—he was no match for the Daito-ryu master. Immediately forgetting about everything else, Morihei stayed at the inn studying with Sokaku for a month (the folks back in Shirataki thought he had perished in a blizzard), the minimum requirement for the *shoden mokuroku* certificate of 118 basic techniques.* Upon his return home, Morihei built a *dojo* on his property and invited Sokaku to live there. In 1917, Morihei began accompanying Sokaku on teaching tours, having sent his family back to Tanabe in Wakayama because of the intense cold.

In 1919, word came from Tanabe that seventy-six-year-old Yoroku was gravely ill; Morihei sold off some of his property in Shirataki, turned the remainder over to Sokaku, and left Hokkaido for good. On the way back to his hometown—a good ten-day

* The oft-repeated story of Morihei paying 300 to 500 yen (equivalent to several hundred of today's dollars) for each technique is certainly false; according to Daito-ryu sources, the standard entrance fee in those days was 3 to 5 yen, and 10 yen was charged for ten days of study. What Morihei likely meant was that the great cost of privately studying with Sokaku in Hokkaido and later Ayabe —Sokaku's transportation, lodging, food, plus the voluntary donation of the Shirataki property— added up to that amount for each technique.

trip in those days—Morihei impulsively stopped at Ayabe, headquarters of the new Omoto-kyo religion he had recently heard so much about, to request a prayer service for the recovery of his father's health. There he met Deguchi Onisaburo, the "Master" of the religion, who told him, "Your father is better off where he is going."

The other-worldly atmosphere of the Ayabe compound enthralled Morihei and he lingered there for three days before resuming his journey. When he arrived home, he found that his father had indeed departed for "a better place" as Onisaburo had predicted. Sorely distressed and terribly confused, Morihei hardly ate or slept for the next three months; every night he would take to the mountains and swing his sword madly until daybreak. Finally, he announced his intention to sell the ancestral land, move to Ayabe, and study Omoto-kyo.

Like many of Japan's new religions, Omoto-kyo, "The Teaching of the Great Origin," was a mixture of Shinto mythology, shamanism, faith-healing, and personality cult. Then at the height of its popularity, with over two million adherents, it was founded by Deguchi Nao, a semiliterate farm woman whose early life was nothing but unrelieved misery. Poverty-stricken from birth, she was forced to work as a housemaid at age ten; her marriage to the poorest farmer in a poor village was tragic—of her eight children, three died in infancy, two ran away from home, and two went insane. After her husband died when she was thirty years old, Nao was reduced to selling rags for a living. In 1892 she had a "revelation" from Tenchi-kane-no-kame, the Great God of the Universe, that a messiah was coming to establish a Kingdom of God on earth and that she must be his prophetess.

In 1898, Nao met clever young Ueda Kisaburo, who claimed he had once left his body, toured every region of the spiritual world, and learned all the secrets of the cosmos. Nao recognized Kisaburo (who later changed his name to Onisaburo) as the promised savior, and after Onisaburo married Nao's daughter Sumiko, they started a religious sect together.

When Moreihei announced his decision to move to Ayabe and study Omoto-kyo, all of his friends and family, including his wife, thought he was crazy. Nonetheless, he would not be deterred, and in the spring of 1920 he and his family rented a house near the Omoto-kyo head shrine. (This year was undoubtedly the most trying of Morihei's life. In addition to his father's death and the painful decision to abandon his home in Tanabe, both of his sons, three-year-old Takamori and one-year-old Kuniji, caught a virus and died within three weeks of each other. His sole surviving son, Kisshomaru, was born in 1921.)

For the next eight years Morihei served as Onisaburo's assistant, taught *budo* at the "Ueshiba Juku," headed the local fire brigade, farmed, and studied the doctrines of Omoto-kyo, especially *chinkon-kishin*, "calming the spirit and returning to the divine."

A pacifist, Onisaburo was an advocate of nonviolent resistance and universal disarmament who once said, "Armament and war are the means by which landlords and capitalists make their profit, while the poor must suffer; there is nothing in the world more harmful than war and more foolish than armament." Why did he welcome the martial artist Morihei, building a *dojo* for him and telling young Omoto followers to study there? Onisaburo realized that Morihei's purpose on earth was "to teach the real meaning of *budo*: an end to all fighting and contention."

Onisaburo was in constant trouble with the authorities because of his pacifist stance and his serious belief that since he was savior of the world, he should be declared emperor and allowed to run the government. In 1921, he was arrested on the charge of *lèse majesté*, but released a few months later during the general amnesty issued at the death of Emperor Taisho.

In 1924, Onisaburo hatched a bizarre scheme to set up a "Heavenly Kingdom on Earth" in Mongolia, site of the "New Jerusalem," with the aid of several Chinese and Korean syncretic religious groups. Once the great spiritual traditions of Asia were united, he believed, the rest of the world could be organized into an association of love and brotherhood under his own direction. Since Onisaburo was under continual police surveillance, the five-man party, including Morihei acting as bodyguard, set out in utmost

Morihei in 1933, age fifty.

secrecy. Arriving in China in February, Onisaburo announced himself as the Dalai Lama incarnation of Maitreya Buddha for whom everyone was waiting. His Chinese hosts were not impressed, and only after great difficulty and many adventures (in which Morihei's ability to dodge bullets came in most handy), did they near their destination. However, the group had somehow alarmed the local warlords, who had them promptly arrested, placed in leg-irons, and taken to an execution ground to be shot. Fortunately, the Japanese consul intervened and the savior and his party were saved at the last second. The members of this fanciful expedition returned to a hero's welcome in July of the same year.

(Onisaburo, his wife, and fifty of his closest followers were arrested in 1935 and sentenced to life imprisonment; all the Omoto buildings were dynamited and the entire movement suppressed. Onisaburo was released on bail in 1942, and spent the remaining six years of his life studying, composing poetry, and making pottery. Omoto-kyo was revived following the war, but has never recovered from the death of

the charismatic Onisaburo; present membership is perhaps two hundred thousand.)

The study of Omoto-kyo and his association with Onisaburo profoundly affected Morihei's life. Even his relationship with Sokaku was influenced. In 1922, Morihei invited Sokaku to Ayabe for a six-month stay, and Sokaku gave him permission to act as an instructor (*shihandai*) of Daito-ryu Aiki-jutsu. (The relationship between Daito-ryu Aiki-jutsu and Aikido is difficult to clearly assess. There were at least twenty others who were given teaching licenses by Sokaku and Morihei never formally received the "complete transmission" [*soden*] of Daito-ryu techniques.) Morihei stated that while Sokaku opened his eyes to the essence of *budo*, his enlightenment came through his Omoto-kyo experiences. Reportedly, Onisaburo advised Morihei to start his own tradition since Daito-ryu methods were too combat-oriented and could not serve as a means to unite man with god and promote harmony among all people. Right from the start, the two systems differed greatly in both their approach and execution. Nonetheless, Sokaku continued to visit Morihei almost every year until his death in 1943, even after Morihei had his own training center in Tokyo. Morihei always footed the bill, treating Sokaku with all the respect due one's master, albeit without enthusiasm.

His close calls in China with Onisaburo also had a great effect on Morihei. Upon his return to Ayabe, he trained more intently than ever, arming his disciples with live swords and commanding them to try to cut him in half. Something was up in the spiritual world, too; every morning at eleven o'clock, the living room of Morihei's house would shake violently as an unearthly sound emitted from the household shrine, and every evening at nine o'clock a tremendous "whoosh" was heard as if some huge object was passing by.

One spring day in 1925, a *kendo* instructor wishing to test Morihei's reputation paid a visit to the Ayabe *dojo*. Relying on his sixth sense—"a flash of light indicated the direction of the attack"—Morihei easily avoided the cuts and thrusts of the instructor's wooden sword. After he left, Morihei went out into his garden to rest. Suddenly he felt bathed in a heavenly light; the ground quaked as a golden cloud welled up from the earth and entered his body. Morihei imagined that he was transformed into a golden being that filled space; the barrier between the spiritual and material worlds had crumbled—"I am the universe." He realized that the true purpose of *budo* was love, love that cherishes and nourishes all beings. Morihei was then forty-two years old.

The Ueshiba Juku in Ayabe was originally intended for Omoto-kyo devotees, but as Morihei's fame spread many nonbelievers, mostly military men, applied for admission. The case of Tomiki Kenji, *judoka* and later founder of the Tomiki system of Aikido, was typical. When a couple of his friends, students of Morihei, urged him to meet their master, Tomiki scoffed and said, "I've heard about Ueshiba and his fake demonstrations; if I take on an over-the-hill forty-year-old all my colleagues will laugh at me." They promised not to reveal the meeting to anyone so Tomiki agreed. Tomiki was introduced and moved confidently toward Morihei, but instantly found himself pinned to the floor. He requested another chance, this time vowing to give it his all. He ended up on the other side of the *dojo*, sprang up and rushed again; after hitting the deck for a second time, he bowed and said, "I hope to become your disciple."

Morihei spent much of 1925-26 in Tokyo teaching at the request of Admiral Takeshita and other influential people. The strain of so much travel and training took its toll; Morihei passed out after a practice session and the doctor prescribed complete rest. (Even though Morihei was occasionally physically ill, he still was able to freely perform his *aiki* techniques. *Aiki* is perhaps the ultimate example of mind over matter. *Ki*-power is never diminished, and does not depend on one's physical condition. For example, near the end of his life, Sokaku insisted on conducting his regular training sessions despite the fact that his right side was paralyzed from a stroke, and it is said that while on his death-bed he threw a six-degree *judoka*.)

After a six-month stay in Ayabe, Morihei's health returned. Onisaburo encouraged Morihei to separate himself from the Omoto-kyo organization, move to Tokyo, and found his own unique "Way." In 1927, Morihei and his family rented a house in Sarumachi in Tokyo's Shiba Shirogane district, and Morihei held

classes in the remodeled billiard room of Prince Shimazu, one of his early supporters. In 1928, Morihei moved to larger quarters in Mita, and then in the following year to a still larger place in Kuruma-machi. Because the number of applicants continued to increase, land was acquired for a formal *dojo* and residence in Ushigome (present site of the headquarters *dojo*).

While the new *dojo* was being constructed, Kano Jigoro paid a visit to Morihei's temporary training hall in Mejiro. After witnessing Morihei's *aiki* techniques Jigoro declared, "This is my ideal *budo*—true *judo*." He dispatched several of his top Kokodan pupils to study with Morihei; one of them, Mochizuki Minoru, later developed his own Aikido-style system.

In 1931, the *dojo* in Ushigome, called the "Kobukan," was finished. (Shirata Sensei became an *uchi-deshi* later this year.) A "Budo Enhancement Society" was founded in 1932 with Morihei as chief instructor. Shioda Gozo, present head of Yoshikan Aikido, became a disciple around the same time. There has always been a close relationship between Aikido and swordsmanship—Sokaku and Morihei were likely the two best swordsmen of the day—and for a time there was a *kendo* division at the Kobukan. Morihei, evidently concerned that his bookworm son Kisshomaru would not be up to succeeding him, adopted a young swordsman named Tanaka Kiyoshi into the Ueshiba family, but he left a few years later for unspecified reasons.

Up to the outbreak of World War II, Morihei was extremely busy teaching at the Kobukan as well as holding special classes at the major military and police academies (he also gave lessons to actors, dancers, and *sumo* wrestlers). Here are a few of the many interesting stories handed down from that period:

The famous general Miura, a hero of the Russo-Japanese War, used to be a student of Daito-ryu and heard about Morihei from Sokaku. One day he noticed the "Ueshiba Dojo" signboard and went in to see what his "fellow-disciple" had to offer. Although Miura was cynical at first, he was impressed by the different emphasis in Ueshiba Aiki-jutsu and decided to study with Morihei. However, still not completely convinced of Morihei's ability,

Miura arranged a training session at Toyama Military Academy. The students of *jukendo* (bayonet fighting) there were noted for their ferocity, size, and strength. They urged Morihei to wear protective armor because things might get a little rough; Morihei declined, saying, "You are using wooden bayonets, so don't worry. Will you attack one-by-one?"

"Of course," was the reply.

"In my *budo*, we always expect attacks from all sides. Please come in a group." Disbelieving, only one student stepped forward. When the others saw him land on his rear end, they lost their reserve and moved in together. No one came close to touching Morihei.

A similar incident occurred at the Military Police Academy. The trainees there were particularly ruthless, and one day thought of surprising their instructor. Usually, twenty to thirty students attended the sessions, but this time only one person showed up. Morihei gave a short lesson, and walked out into the open courtyard to return home. All at once, the members of the class, armed with wooden swords, sticks, and bayonets swarmed out to "greet" Morihei. In his customary unruffled manner, he deftly avoided their attacks and passed through the gate as if nothing had happened.

At the central police headquarters in Osaka, Morihei was giving a class, and asked five of the biggest officers to pin him on the floor —one on top with a choke hold, and one on each limb. Although Morihei's entire body was under the weight of the policemen, in an instant they were thrown off. Observers noticed hardly any movement, and when they questioned the men holding Morihei down, they were told, "His body was as soft as silk when we first held it; as he emitted a short *kiai* he became like a piece of iron and we flew off." The man with the choke hold mentioned that he felt his hands being wrenched off Morihei's neck. Morihei laughed as he chided them, "You'd better learn more effective arrest techniques if you are going to deal with dangerous criminals."

Morihei told his *uchi-deshi* that if they ever caught him off guard even for a moment, he would treat them all to a grand feast. Day and night, the disciples tried to sneak up on him to

no avail; even when he was sleeping, as soon as they got near Morihei he stirred. Actually, they thought he was not sleeping at all and was perhaps suffering from some neurotic disorder so they summoned a doctor to examine him. "I feel fine," said Morihei. "Why did you call a doctor?" They related the details of their nightly missions; since he did not seem to be resting well they presumed he was ill. "I was sound asleep," Morihei assured them. "Invisible rays emanate from my body and whenever anyone comes within ten or fifteen feet of me I can immediately sense his presence even in my sleep." In a similar vein, Shirata Sensei recalls that he and the other young *uchi-deshi* occasionally slipped out to enjoy a modest "night on the town." Even though Morihei's room was quite far from the *dojo* gate and the disciples took every precaution not to make any noise, invariably the next morning the Founder would ask, "Where did you fellows go last night?"

One day Morihei was riding on a crowded train with several of his disciples. The man next to him suddenly froze with a strange expression on his face; Morihei apparently knew the man, his disciples thought, since he was smiling. At the next stop, Morihei said, "Scram!" and the man ran off the train. "Who was that?" his students asked. "A pickpocket," Morihei told them.

Speaking of trains, Morihei was probably the most demanding traveler in the country. He insisted on being at the station at least an hour before the train was scheduled to depart, which was not so bad; much worse was his disconcerting habit of boarding the train with his luggage and several attendants only to leap up just before the train left the station and declare, "Get off this train! I'm not going anywhere!" The disciples had no choice but to obey his orders. A few minutes after the last train pulled away, he would say, "I feel better now. Let's go." Hypersensitive to the slightest change in mood, Morihei frequently, and capriciously, altered his plans. His disciples never knew what to expect—Morihei's method of keeping them alert?—and he would not stand for inattentive or halfhearted behavior on their part.

One of Morihei's earliest disciples was Niki Kenzo, "Doctor Brown Rice," an advocate of health food. Although Morihei did not care much for brown rice—he had trouble digesting it—he did prefer plain and simple food: vegetables and fish. His secret weapon was chicken soup; whenever he felt out-of-sorts he drank a bowl. Unlike the majority of *budoka*, Morihei almost never drank sake.

His disciples once asked Morihei if the feats attributed to *ninja*—e.g., becoming invisible, walking on water—were actually done. "You have been watching too many movies," Morihei said. "Grab your swords and sticks and I'll give you a real demonstration of *ninjutsu*." Ten or so of them surrounded Morihei in the center of the *dojo*, and as soon as they attacked, they felt a stream of air and Morihei disappeared. "Over here, over here!" they heard Morihei calling from half way up the second story stairs twenty feet away. Later, however, Morihei got quite upset when they asked him to do some more *ninja* "tricks." "Are you trying to kill me just to entertain yourselves? Each time one performs such techniques, his life span is reduced five to ten years."

Yet even Morihei lost his footing. Kisshomaru remembers well an incident that occurred when he was a primary school student. He got into a fight with an American boy who lived nearby; the boy started throwing stones, and Morihei, who sensed something wrong, ran out into the street, but slipped in a puddle, allowing the boy to escape. To this day,

Kisshomaru is unsure whether Morihei was furious at the American boy for hurling rocks or at his son—then a rather weak and spiritless child—for shrinking from the challenge.

If Morihei's *budo* stood for love and peace, what was his attitude toward the "Great East Asian War"? Unlike Onisaburo, who never abandoned his pacifist principles and went to prison for his beliefs, Morihei appeared to be an ardent supporter of the Imperial cause. He taught at the major military academies, many of his disciples were among those directing the war, he went to Manchuria as a guest of the puppet government there, and so on. Yet Kisshomaru has written that both prior to and during the war, he heard his father complain bitterly, "The military is dominated by reckless fools ignorant of statesmanship and religious ideals who slaughter innocent citizens indiscriminately and destroy everything in their path. They act in total contradiction to God's will, and will surely come to a sorry end. True *budo* is to nourish life and foster peace, love, and respect, not to blast the world to pieces with weapons." Morihei hinted that his move to the Iwama outdoor *dojo* in 1942 was prompted by a "divine command"; he foresaw that the war would not end well for Japan and hoped that Aikido would become the creed of a new era.

The war had emptied the Kobukan *dojo* and Morihei, tired of city life and the burdens of administering a large center, longed to

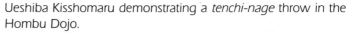

Ueshiba Kisshomaru demonstrating a *tenchi-nage* throw in the Hombu Dojo.

Morihei at prayer. Taken during his 1961 instruction tour of Hawaii.

place of Aiki-do, "The Way of Harmony." Prior to Morihei's move there, his system was called Aiki-jutsu, then Aiki-budo, still primarily arts rather than spiritual paths. During the years from 1942—when the name Aikido was first formally used—to 1952, Morihei consolidated the techniques and perfected the religious philosophy of Aikido.

In the aftermath of Japan's surrender in 1945, his disciples believed that Aikido would cease to exist, but Morihei was confident that, on the contrary, Aikido would flourish and its true value become known all over the world. In 1948, the "Aikikai" (Aiki Association) was formed to promote Aikido in Japan and abroad. Morihei left the organizing to his son and top disciples, preferring to pursue further training in Iwama. He rose every morning at 5 o'clock (3 o'clock on feast days), prayed and meditated for several hours, and then either farmed or studied depending on the weather. Every evening he led the training sessions. Saito Morihiro, present head of the Iwama Dojo, recalls: "When the Founder meditated the air was permeated by an intense, grave spirituality, but when he finished we felt the warmth of his love and compassion." Farming and Aikido were his life and the entire world his *dojo*.

The rapid spread of Aikido after the war under the direction of the Hombu Dojo, now headquartered in a three-story building in Tokyo, is a well-known story. Morihei became world-famous as "O-Sensei," the master of Aikido, and received a number of decorations from the Japanese government.

Right to the end of his life, Morihei refined and improved his techniques, never losing his dedication to hard training. In the early spring of 1969, Morihei fell ill, and told Kisshomaru that "God is calling me..." Hospitalized, Morihei's condition was diagnosed as cancer of the liver. (All through his life Morihei had had frequent liver and stomach trouble. He blamed it on a salt-water drinking contest he had with a Japanese yoga practitioner who was pestering Onisaburo or one of the Omoto-kyo believers to take the challenge. A more likely cause was excessively hard training.) He was returned home at his request to be near his *dojo*. Even though he was no longer able to physically conduct the practices, he could tell

return to the land where he could ideally combine *budo* and farming, two things that created life and purified the heart. He often said that "*Budo* and farming are one." Morihei placed the city *dojo* in the hands of his son, resigned his official positions, and left Tokyo with his wife to settle on their property, purchased some years previously, in the village of Iwama in Ibaragi Prefecture. Morihei lived there quietly for the remainder of the war, practicing, studying, farming, and supervising the construction of the Aiki Shrine and Shuren Dojo. Iwama may be considered the birth-

exactly what was going on by listening to the sounds in the *dojo*. Those with him said he was never stronger—his body had wasted away to almost nothing, but he was so heavy ten of his most powerful disciples were unable to lift him.

On April 15, Morihei's condition became critical; as his many disciples and friends made their final calls, he gave his last instructions: "Aikido is for the entire world. Train not for selfish reasons, but for all people everywhere." Early on the morning of April 26, the eighty-six-year-old Morihei took his son's hand, smiled, said "Take care of things," and died. Two months later to the day, Hatsu, his wife of sixty-seven years, followed him.

Morihei's ashes were buried in the family temple in Tanabe, and parts of his hair were enshrined in Ayabe, in the Aiki Shrine, and in the Kumano Juku Dojo (headed by Hikitsuchi Michio). Every year a memorial service is held on April 29 at the Aiki Shrine in Iwama.

Eighty-year-old Morihei performing the "divine techniques" of Aikido.

Memorial demonstration (*embu*) at the Aiki shrine being performed by current *Doshu* Ueshiba Kisshomaru. He succeeded his father as Head Master after Morihei's death in 1969. Kisshomaru's son and heir apparent Moriteru watches from the side. To Moriteru's left is Shirata Sensei and to his right is Ozawa Sensei, chief instructor of the Hombu Dojo.

The Aiki shrine in Iwama, Ibaraki Prefecture.

Every April 29, a memorial service is held for the Founder at the Aiki shrine.

2

Fifty Years
of Aikido

Shirata Rinjiro was born in 1912 in the northern prefecture of Yamagata. A descendant of the famous ninth century scholar Sugawara Michizane—later deified as Temma Tenjin, the patron saint of learning—his ancestors were mainly government ministers and *samurai*, but following the abolition of the feudal system in 1871, the Shirata family engaged in agriculture and forestry. Shirata Sensei's father, however, retained a strong interest in the *samurai* tradition and constructed a *kendo* training hall on his property. Shirata Sensei began *kendo* as an elementary school student, but later switched to *judo* in middle school, quickly attaining the rank of *ni-dan*. His father became acquainted with Ueshiba Morihei through Omoto-kyo, and decided that his unusually powerful son—the boy could easily lift a one hundred thirty pound bag of rice with one hand—should study with that master.

After his graduation from middle school in 1931, his father took him to Tokyo to request admission to the recently opened Kobukan *dojo*. Shirata Sensei recalls the initial meeting with the Founder well. "Although the Founder was quite short, tremendous energy radiated from his barrel chest and thick stomach muscles. He smiled and laughed continually, but his glare was fierce and penetrating. There were two girl trainees about my age [nineteen years old] present, and the Founder told me to try to throw one of them. Despite my knowledge of *judo* and my superior build, I was no match for her—she kept whipping me to the mat with a painful technique I later learned was *shiho-nage*. After this humbling experience, I petitioned the Founder to become his student." (One of the girls, Kumikoshi Takako, is still living and has achieved some success as an artist.)

Throughout the history of Aikido, women have practiced together with men under the same conditions on the same level.

"It was extremely difficult to get permission to enter in those days," Shirata Sensei continues, "Two trustworthy sponsors were required and anyone with an improper attitude was immediately rejected. Consequently, there were never more than a few *uchi-deshi*. There was no regular tuition system—when asked about the 'charge' for the lessons, the Founder would thunder, 'I'm not teaching you for money!' So once accepted, a cash donation was placed on the *dojo* altar, and thereafter each student and his family contributed whatever they could. In my case, my father supplied the master with rice and other staples. Even after admission, I was not allowed to join in the training for some months; I could only watch and take care of the cleaning and other chores."

After the probationary period, the trainee acted as an *uke* for the advanced students, doing nothing but taking falls and being pinned. It was often six months or more before a newcomer was able to test a technique himself. Because the entire country was preparing for future military adventures, the training was particularly severe. In addition to three practices a day, there were many outside training sessions as well as special demonstrations. Also, because the Founder's system at that time—known variously as Daito-ryu Aiki-jutsu, Aiki-budo, Kobukan-judo, Ueshiba-ryu jujutsu, etc.—was primarily an art rather than a "way," practical application was highly emphasized. (Even today, that realistic, "combative" quality can be discerned in Shirata Sensei's techniques; in the post-war years the Founder's movements became much more free-flowing.) The Kobukan indeed deserved its nickname—"The Hell Dojo."

Each practice began and ended with breathing techniques. The Founder often illustrated his explanations with different weapons, especially the sword and wooden bayonet. Every body technique was explained in terms of sword movements and entering thrusts.

The Founder was in his late forties then, perhaps at the peak of his physical strength. Shirata Sensei was amazed at his power: "Although his hand was tiny, half the size of my own, his grip was crushing; it was impossible to move when he held your arm and even when he pinned you with one finger there would be a bruise on the spot for days. I could never comprehend how he threw us—all of a sudden you were flying through the air, almost as if floating on a cloud. You rarely felt knocked down. On the other hand, whenever he pinned you, it was like receiving an electric shock, the pain was so intense. The Founder was most terrifying when holding a sword; his countenance was utterly transformed. He looked like some ferocious demon warrior."

Even among such a select group of trainees, Shirata Sensei became known as the "Marvel of the Kobukan," especially after his year-long stay in Okayama Prefecture. In 1934 Shirata Sensei was sent to establish a branch of the Budo Enhancement Society there. In Tokyo, the forbidding presence of the Founder discouraged all but the most foolhardy challengers, but in the provinces many were eager to test the skill of his young disciples. *Judo* men, *kendo* men, *sumo* wrestlers, boxers, and just plain brawlers came forth to compete with the new instructor. Shirata Sensei informed them that there is "no fighting in Aikido because *shiai* (contest) really means *shiai* (mutual killing)." Nonetheless, he rose to meet any attack; more than one arm was broken, and no one was able to boast of besting the nonfighter. "Who can resist the power of nonresistance?" he joked as he pinned one braggart.

Unfortunately, it is not possible to relate the episodes in more detail. Whenever I ask him about these famous incidents, Shirata Sensei simply says, "Such things happen," and then adds with a smile, "I was pretty strong in those days." (He did say once, however, that *shiho-nage*, the *irimi* movements, and the *ikkyo* and *nikyo* pins were the most effective techniques, and that in event of trouble one should not stand still and wait for an attack, as in regular practice. Especially against someone armed with a weapon, to stop and assume a static posture is to be defeated.) It is true that some of his opponents were injured, but that occur-

red because they unnaturally resisted nonresistance; Shirata Sensei never reacted violently or applied more force than necessary. Much more recently, a karate man, claiming the desire to learn Aikido, attempted to cross up Shirata Sensei by delivering a kick rather than the standard straight blow to the head. Shirata Sensei cleanly stepped to the side, laughed, and gently upended the upstart.

In the early days there was no *dan-kyu* ranking system; the Founder followed the traditional system of presenting disciples with a certificate when he was satisfied with their progress. The four levels were: (1) *kirikami*; (2) *mokuroku*; (3) *menkyo*; (4) *kaiden*. Shirata Sensei received *mokuroku*, "the catalogue of techniques" and does not know if anyone else was presented with one of the higher certificates ("It was none of my business," he says). But that is doubtful since it is difficult to imagine anyone more advanced.

In 1937, Shirata Sensei was drafted into the army and later served as an officer in Man-

Shirata Sensei (the burly young man standing in the middle of the second row) and the other *uchi-deshi* of the Kobukan Dojo. Taken around 1932 when he was twenty years old.

churia and Burma. He was a prisoner of war briefly before being repatriated in 1946. He never talks about his war experiences—like all good masters he lives in the present—except to say, "During the war we were told that *Bushido* means to learn how to die. I learned that this is not real *budo*; real *budo* is to learn how to live, how to live together with others in harmony and peace."

After a nine-year hiatus, Shirata Sensei resumed his study with the Founder in both Tokyo and Iwama. In 1949, Shirata Sensei became an insurance agent, married, and returned to his native district to work, raise three children, and teach Aikido. Semiretired from business, Shirata Sensei is currently Director of the All-Japan Aikido Association, Chairman of the International Aikido Review Committee, and Head Instructor of Northern Japan.

There is no finer testament to the health-promoting qualities of Aikido than Shirata Sensei. Now in his early seventies, his extraordinary vigor is the envy of those half his age. Once at a special training session he threw me around for two solid hours before whispering (in the nick of time), "You must be tired. Take a rest." He then called on another two-hundred-pounder to replace me for the remaining hour of practice. Shirata Sensei often says happily, "How I love to practice with these youngsters!"

Aikido, of course, is much more than physical culture; in fact, the real practice of Aikido is said to begin when one's raw power is on the wane. The Founder stated that he did not enter the realm of pure Aikido until he was near eighty. As Shirata Sensei relies more and more on "*ki*" and "breath" power, his techniques become sharper and more effective; there has been a marked improvement in the last ten years. In stark contrast to competitive sports where most forty-year-olds are "washed up," one can only get better with age in Aikido.

Paradoxically, such stamina is not developed by conserving one's energy. Every time Shirata Sensei performs a technique it is a *shinken shobu*, a "fight to the death." That is, every ounce of physical and spiritual strength is concentrated on the "here" and "now" of the Aikido encounter. If anything is held back or if there are distracting thoughts, there will be

no progress of any kind. It is frequently said that ten minutes of training with complete extension of body and mind is more valuable than ten hours of mechanically going through the motions.

This is the reason it is always better for practitioners to have some other occupation besides Aikido. Throwing and pinning are only one aspect of Aikido training, and too much time in the *dojo* destroys the balance between practice, work, study, and social obligations. Shirata Sensei is still only semiretired, and although the Founder taught fulltime in Tokyo for some years, he far preferred to combine Aikido with farm work. Also, because of the Founder's example, it is not really proper to teach for money. It can be accepted (with gratitude) when offered, but is not advisable to make a living at Aikido.

Like the Founder who maintained, "I'm still a beginner," Shirata Sensei retains the enthusiasm and determination of a new student. Recently he said to us, "I'm finally getting the hang of *shiho-nage*." Since Shirata Sensei, associated with Aikido from its inception, has been a keen observer of the many changes that have occurred over the years, he can best answer the questions that trouble every serious Aikido practitioner: Why are there so many different "Aikido" systems if everyone originally had the same master? Why does the performance of a technique vary so greatly from instructor to instructor even in the same *dojo*? What is the real Aikido? Whose techniques are correct?

Shirata Sensei explains, "Throughout his life, the Founder continually refined the approach and execution of his techniques. This is quite natural because Aikido techniques are not, as many mistakenly believe, *kata*—fixed forms that have been handed down from the past and must be preserved unaltered—but 'living,' infinitely varied responses to a particular situation. Therefore, every generation of disciples was exposed to a different type of Aikido, and within each generation each student had his or her own interpretation reflecting individual levels of progress, attitude, and extent of spiritual insight. For example, the 'Aikido' of my fellow disciples—Tomiki, Mochizuki, Shioda—differs from each other and from my own. Each one of us focused on what we thought most important. In my fifty years of Aikido training, I have tried to faithfully preserve the essence of what I learned from the Founder. Yet the way I express that essence in my techniques has changed as my understanding of the Founder's message has deepened. Because the scope of that message is so vast and the forms in which it was expressed so great, no one can confidently state that a particular style is the 'real' Aikido or that there is a single Aikido standard. There can never be rigid uniformity in Aikido, but we must guard against totally ignoring the Founder's message to set up pseudo-Aikido based on personal quirks. If we keep the spirit of the Founder in our hearts and train sincerely, surely the Way of Harmony will open for us."

Shirata Sensei is a real *shihan*, "model teacher." Devoted to the spirit of the Founder, still enthusiastically studying after fifty years of training, free of jealousy and criticism toward other instructors, indifferent to material gain, a man of peace and mature wisdom, he embodies the best qualities of a true Aikido practitioner.

3

The Heart
of Aikido

Thousands of hours went into the development of the techniques, but thousands more were spent struggling with the great matters of human existence, and to treat Aikido as a martial art comprised of throws and pins—skills that can be acquired from any system of self-defense—is an insult to the Founder's lifelong spiritual quest.

The Founder's special message, however, cannot be assimilated quickly. He borrowed ideas freely to express his unique vision and his talks were a jumble of esoteric Buddhist phrases, obscure Shinto myths, and cryptic Omoto-kyo doctrines. No one, including the Founder himself, ever claimed to understand them fully and on one occasion he stated: "Words and letters can never adequately describe Aikido—its meaning is revealed only to those who are enlightened through hard training." Shirata Sensei says that although he was at first totally confounded by the Founder's explanations, over the years they have gradually begun to make sense. The following is Shirata Sensei's summary of the key points of the Founder's religious philosophy.

Aikido has its own cosmology. The words *aiki*, *kami*, and *takemusu* are ancient terms, but the Founder reinterpreted them in light of his profound awakening. *Ki* is the primal energy that arose from the Void. Through *aiki*, the blending of positive *ki* and negative *ki* (yin and yang), the myriad forms of phenomena were (and are) manifest. *Aiki*, the source and sustenance of life, is *kami*, the Divine. Originally, this word consisted of the characters *ka* (fire), symbolizing spirit, and *mi* (water), symbolizing matter. Confluence of those two elements resulted in the appearance of the material world. *Kami* functions as *iki* (*kokyu*), the vivifying breath of life. From *iki* arises *kotodama*, the "divine vibrations" of name and form. To these two procreative forces, the Founder added a third, *takemusu,* the "valor of active being." *Take,* ("martial ardor") also pronounced *"bu"* (as in *budo*), is tireless diligence; *musu* is *musubi,* the power of becoming.

The Founder's grand perception of the universe is "Takemusu Aiki." On the highest level, Takemusu Aiki may be interpreted in this manner: "Bu is born from Aiki; Bu gives birth to Aiki." In human perspective, "I was born from my parents; I gave birth to my parents." That is to say, "I am Aiki; I am the universe."

In more concrete terms: *Aiki* is first applied to harmonize the three functions of body, mind, and *ki.* After that we use *aiki* to blend our movements with that of our partner when we perform the techniques. In this case, *aiki* is *a-i-ki,* represented by a triangle, a circle, and a square, the basic patterns of creation. The motions in Aikido follow these patterns, e.g., triangular stance, circular entry, square control (it must be remembered that the techniques are not *aiki; aiki* operates through the techniques). Once these harmonizations are accomplished—no easy matter—it is necessary to put ourselves in tune with the environment, adjusting naturally to its changes. (That is why *dojos* in Japan are never cooled or heated.) Eventually, we imperceptibly merge with the universe, incorporating its dynamism as our own. This entire process is *kimusubi,* linking *ki* to promote life.

Aiki unifies body and mind, self and others, matter and spirit, man and the universe. In his last years, the Founder suggested that *"ai"* (harmony) be replaced by *"ai"* (love) since love is the highest form of harmony: it nourishes all things and brings them to fulfillment. "Love is the guardian deity of all beings; without love nothing can flourish. The Way of Aiki is an expression of love. . . . Love does not hate, love has nothing to oppose it. Love is God's essence."

Kami-sama, "God," was the phrase the Founder used to represent the Ultimate, the Absolute, the Universal Spirit of Love and Harmony. *Hito,* the Japanese word for human being is composed of *hi,* the spark of life, that has *to,* stopped temporarily in this vessel we call our body. The *"ka"* of *kami* and the *"hi"* of *hito* are the same character—if there is no *kami* there is no *hito* and vice versa. That is why the Founder insisted that, "A human being is the child of God, a living shrine of the Divine."

Aiki Okami, "The Great Spirit of Aiki," is the supreme symbol of those ideals the Founder esteemed most highly. Through devoted practice of Aikido techniques—functions of the Divine— it is possible to progress toward that exalted state. Indeed, we ourselves can become *kami,* a perfected human being. A *kami* is not some kind of supernatural creature, but an individual who has uncovered his or her true nature—none other than the universe itself—through constant effort. "Aikido is the Way of God; establishing the power of Aiki builds the strength of divine activity."

The power of divine activity is none other

Calligraphy of "Takemusu Aiki" by the Founder.

than Takemusu Aiki. Heretofore, *take* stood for the law of the jungle: "If I don't kill him, he will kill me." Such an attitude is contrary to the survival of humankind. The Founder realized that *take* is not for destruction and death, but for life and light. The intensity and single-minded determination of the warrior must be channeled toward a higher purpose: "the restoration of harmony, the preservation of peace, and the nurturing of all beings." Shirata Sensei believes that the Founder was a divine messenger sent here to warn us foolish human beings of the futility of waging war and killing each other. "*Aiki* is not an art for defeating others; it is for the unification of the world and the gathering of all races into one family."

Above all, Aikido is *misogi*, the Great Way of Purification. Since we are endowed with life we are divine, but due to imperfections and base thoughts, our true nature is obscured. Instead of using water to wash off impurities, we use the pristine techniques of Aikido—every cut of the sword, every thrust of the *jo*, every movement of the body, is an act of expelling evil and cleansing the heart. *Misogi* is the process of driving off wickedness, purging the body of defilements, and polishing the spirit. As the layers of foulness and corruption are worn away, our immaculate inner light shines brighter and brighter.*

The Founder's spiritual legacy—how to live in divine harmony with the world and all its inhabitants, full of indomitable power and creative love—must be sought out in sincere Aikido training.

Aiki Okami, "The Great Spirit of Aiki."

* Although Aikido is sometimes referred to as "moving Zen," it is clear from the above account that it is much more deeply rooted in Shintoism than Zen Buddhism. Contrary to popular belief, the Founder never formally studied or practiced Zen and rarely mentioned it in his talks. D.T. Suzuki, who knew the Founder well, considered Aikido to be a form of "Oriental enlightenment" expressed in a traditional Japanese framework. Since Zen and Aikido therefore both originate from the same source, their principles are essentially parallel. Nonetheless, certain attitudes are completely different and no attempt should be made to artificially combine the two disciplines.

4

Aikido Training

The motto of Aikido training is *Masakatsu Akatsu*, "By acting in accordance with the truth we always emerge victorious."

We train formally in a *dojo*. Originally this word (Sanskrit: *bodhimanda*) referred to the area of Shakyamuni Buddha's enlightenment; now it is applied to any training hall where a Way is practiced. As a holy place of learning and determined effort, it must be kept clean and free of distractions. Everything must be as simple as possible. Behave no differently in a *dojo* than you would in a church or a temple. Always bow upon entering and leaving.

Prior to practice a twenty-minute or so warm-up session is advised to prepare both the body and mind. The body should be sufficiently stretched to prevent injuries and the mind sufficiently calmed to foster clear vision. In addition to the standard Aikido warm-up exercises, Shirata Sensei recommends a full cycle of breath-meditation (see following section).

Training partners should always be approached with gratitude and respect. Aikido is the Way of gentlemen and gentlewomen —when we bow to each other we lower our heads all the way to the floor. This is the same bow made before a Shinto altar, a gesture of honor and trust. An exponent of Aikido expects only the highest form of behavior from his fellow practitioners. Unfortunately, we all too often run across misguided individuals, including instructors, who take pride in their ability to smash weaker partners to the mat while refusing to be thrown themselves. (Anyone with a bit of training and some muscular strength can resist easily since one knows in advance what technique will be applied.) We must never shrink from any challenge, and learning to deal with any attack is an important element in our practice. But if there is

The Aikido bow, an expression of gratitude and respect.

nothing but resistance, it will no longer be Aikido. There is no harmony, no love, no *kokyu*, no meaning, in any type of struggle. The purpose of Aikido training is never to acquire mastery over others—one with such a thought is defeated from the beginning—and that is why contests are strictly prohibited. The Founder instructed us to "attack opponents with the power of love; bind them with your affection."

When actually performing the techniques, do not think in terms of subduing your "opponent"; concentrate instead on perfecting your movement (*tai-sabaki*) and coordinating your flow of *ki* and *kokyu* with that of your partner. Pay the most meticulous attention to the development of proper breathing, correct placement of the feet, hips, and hands, maintaining adequate balance, timing, and all the other complex factors involved in each technique. Do not look "at" your partner, but look "through" him or her. Every encounter is a *shinken shobu*, a fight to the death, not of your partner but of your lower self.

If we train sincerely, every day there is progress—a new technique is discovered, an old one handled better, fresh insights occur. This is the path the Founder opened for us; when there is no longer a distinction between daily life and the practice of Aikido we will truly be following the Way of Harmony.

AIKIDO
TECHNIQUES

Study the photographs carefully, noting especially the placement of Shirata Sensei's feet and hips, the extension of his arms, the type of grip he employs, the angle of his *tegatana* (hand-sword), and his concluding *zanshin* posture. These form the essence of a technique and are never executed in a haphazard or sloppy manner. Aikido body-techniques (*taijutsu*) are always practiced from both the right and left, but due to space limitations only one or the other side is shown here. (The directions given for each technique are of course reversed when practicing from the opposite side.) The photo sequences run top to bottom, left to right across the page. In some cases camera perspective is shifted to better illustrate the performance of a technique.

Note: *Atemi* describes the "defensive blow" employed to unbalance an opponent. *Uke* is the one who "receives" the technique.

5

Kokyu-ho:
Breath-Meditation

The Founder once said, "Aikido begins and ends with *kokyu.*" *Kokyu* means "breath" with the special connotation of "being in tune with other people and with one's surroundings"; it also signifies the "knack" or "key point" of a technique or process.

To breathe is to live, and to live is to breathe. Existence starts with an exhalation, the shout of life; when the breath stops, our sojourn here is over. Breath sparks life and vivifies the body; as long as our *kokyu* is deep and steady we will flourish.

Kokyu, however, is not mere mechanical breathing with the lungs; it is the fundamental rhythm of life that energizes and fills the universe. To develop good *kokyu*, we need profound insight into the nature of existence and correct application of certain principles. In Aikido, that is known as *"kokyu-ho," "breath-meditation."*

Makoto no kokyu: True Breath

Fudo no shisei, "immovable posture." In order to breathe properly one must first sit correctly. In the Japanese martial ways, the preferred sitting posture is *seiza*. The distance between each knee and the distance between each knee and the feet should be equal (most practitioners tend to keep the knees too close together). The right big toe is crossed over the left big toe. Pull the chin in, extend the spine, and sit solidly on the buttocks. Gravity should be centered in the triangle formed by your legs and feet and the triangle formed by your knees and head, i.e., in the middle of the lower abdomen about two inches below the navel (*kikai tanden*). This point is also the center of the sphere formed by the two triangles. Although this posture makes one as stable as a mountain, "immovable" does not mean rigid; it indicates an unperturbed mind capable of responding to anything that arises.

1

Ten no kokyu, "the breath of Heaven." In *ten no kokyu, seiki,* the vivifying force of the cosmos is collected within the body; your breath fills the heavens. Close the eyes and exhale deeply. Raise your hands together with the thumbs crossed (left thumb inside), and slowly inhale as if your breath is soaring to the farthest reaches of space. Move the hands in front of the face, and then directly over the head; at the apex of the in-breath when the arms are fully extended and parallel to the ears, turn the hands outward. Now gradually exhale as if the entire sky—sun, moon, stars, clouds—is being pulled by your outstretched arms and fingers into the core of your body. Imagine yourself to be larger than the universe. When the hands touch the mat, turn them out and then bring them together in front of the *tanden.* Repeat three times (after the initial exhalation).

2

5

6

8

9

10

Chi no kokyu, "the breath of Earth." In *chi no kokyu*, the inexhaustible fecundity of the earth is gathered up in the pit of the stomach. Place the hands together, with the left hand on top and the thumbs touching lightly, just below the navel. Exhale once forcefully and root your body to earth by firmly pulling back the shoulders and lowering the diaphragm. Let your shoulders naturally rise as you breathe up everything the land puts forth; exhale by tightening the shoulders and sinking your breath into the depths of the earth. Repeat three times (after the initial exhalation).

1

2

3

4

Jin no kokyu, "the breath of human beings." Human life is the result of the confluence of the breath of Heaven and the breath of earth; we cannot come into being until the two are harmonized. This is *kimusubi*, the blending of heavenly and earthly *ki*, the coming together of the highest and lowest. Continue to sit quietly with the eyes closed and the hands crossed; project yourself into the deepest mountain and most distant valley.

Reside in solitary and serene splendor, abandon all distinctions, and make no conscious effort to inhale or exhale. Merge peacefully with the surroundings and let the breath flow naturally. Ponder the three great questions: Where am I from? Where am I going? What is a human being? *Jin no kokyu* is self-introspection that puts us in touch with the wellspring of life (one to two minutes before practice, longer if sitting alone).

Upon completion of the Heaven-Earth-Human Being breath cycle—a process of unification, purification, and affirmation of life—bow with the utmost gratitude. Form a triangle with the hands, place the forearms directly on the floor, and lower the head until the nose is in the center of the triangle. Exhale on the way down, and inhale when rising.

Keeping the eyes closed, exhale, inhale, exhale, and then quietly open the eyes while inhaling. Skip a breath and gaze off into the distance. Aware of our true nature, with our original vitality restored and our mind purified and settled, the practice of Aikido techniques, in full spirit and proper form, can now commence.

Kokyu-undo: Breath Movement

Following completion of the stationary breathing techniques, *kokyu* is expressed in gradually more active forms.

Suwari kokyu-ho, "sitting breath movement." When a good seed is planted, it does not lie dormant; deriving nourishment from heaven and earth, it throbs with life, overflowing with *kokyu*. It splits in two as a sprout emerges; positively rooted in the earth the sprout dynamically extends itself straight up, breaking through the ground, continually reaching toward the sun. Seemingly pliant and tender, its upward drive is unstoppable; sooner or later it will shatter the hardest surface.

The action in *suwari kokyu-undo* is based on that analogy. The head is the top of the sprout, and the legs are the two halves of the seed. Spread the fingers of both hands like "a pair of blooming flowers" and inhale (either through the mouth or through the nose) while thrusting the arms toward the sky. At the top of the movement, you should be standing on your toes; tuck them under as you exhale and return to the original position. (Repeat eight to ten times.)

Viewed from the front.

Viewed from the side.

Tate kokyu-undo, "standing breath movement." Although sitting and standing appear to be the most fundamental of all postures, it is rare, even among Buddhist priests and martial arts practitioners, to see anyone truly sitting or truly standing. *Fudo no shisei,* "immovable posture," is necessary sitting or standing. To stand, rise on the left knee, vigorously projecting the body slightly forward. Once up, the spine should be straight, the shoulders relaxed, the fingers charged with *ki,* and the gaze open in all directions.

Viewed from the front.

How to stand (side view).

To sit, withdraw the right leg and then bring the left leg back until the feet meet and form a sixty-degree angle; drop straight down, as solidly as a falling boulder.

Standing Kokyu-undo No. 1 There are three ways to practice standing *kokyu-undo*: (1) keeping the same foot forward (always begin with the left); (2) alternating the feet (left-right); and (3) pivoting from left to right. From the waist down you are connected to earth; from the waist up you reach toward heaven. Do not merely swing the arms up and down listlessly; try to pierce the sky with your hands. The breath pattern is up-inhale, down-exhale.

1

2

3

4

Standing Kokyu-undo No. 2

1

2

3

4

5

6

Standing Kokyu-undo No. 3

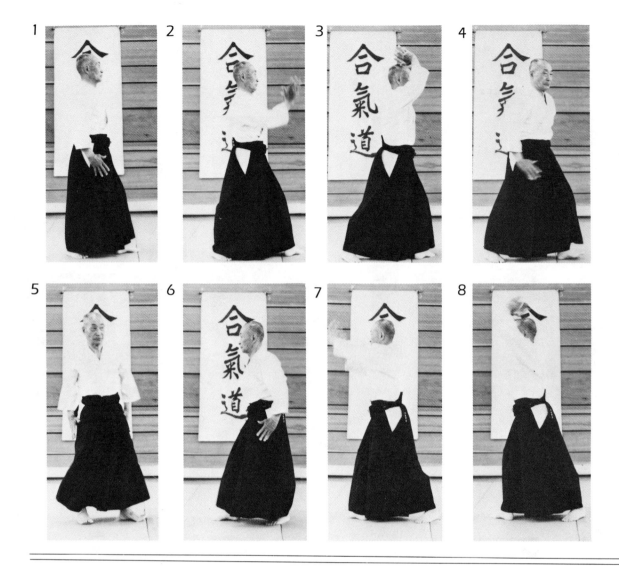

Shikko and Niho-zenshin Zengo-kiri.
Essentially, every Aikido technique is a function of *kokyu*, i.e., a combination of exhalation (*seimei*, "life force") and inhalation (*do*, "activity"). From sitting and standing *kokyu-undo* we proceed on to *ugoku-kokyu*, "moving-breath" and *kokyu-ryoku*, "breath-power."

Since the Founder instructed us to "advance with the left and withdraw with the right" (*sashin-yutai*), the movements begin with the left leg. (As usual, the Founder had an esoteric explanation: *hi*, from *hidari* (left), symbolizes our attraction toward divine light and pure spirit, i.e., progress; *mi*, from *migi* (right), symbolizes our individual body, i.e., regression.)

Shikko, "knee-walking." *Shikko* is an important exercise for strengthening the legs and hips. Keep the center of gravity level as you move, and do not drag the feet or swing excessively from side to side. The buttocks must be kept firmly against the heel(s) at all times. As in sitting and standing *kokyu-undo*, imagine yourself shattering the heavens with your arms on the upward inhalation and cutting through the earth on the downward exhalation. The movements are exactly the same when holding a sword.

Body-technique.

Sword-technique.

Niho-zenshin zengo-kiri, "two steps forward, turn and cut." This basic Aikido movement fosters breath-power and hip stability. Practice with and without a sword. (Only the first half of each cycle is shown.)

No. 1. Body-technique. While inhaling, lift the arms in a circle and bring the hands together over the head; exhale forcefully while bringing them straight down. The complete cycle is: left cut, right cut, turn, left cut, right cut, left cut, turn, right cut. Inhale when raising the arms and exhale when bringing them down.

No. 1. Sword-technique.

No. 2. Body-technique. Left-right cut, turn, left cut, right-left cut, turn, right cut.

No. 2. Sword-technique.

No. 3. Body-technique. Left-right thrust, turn, left cut, right-left thrust, turn, right cut.

At first, each cut should follow the inhale-exhale pattern; later it is necessary to practice completing a cycle in one long breath. That is, inhale deeply on the first up-stroke and then finish the entire cycle while emitting an audible, unbroken exhalation (*kiai*).

No. 3. Sword-technique.

In accordance with the Founder's dictate, Shirata Sensei always begins each practice session with this sequence of breath techniques and ends it with sitting *kokyu-undo*. Aikido breathing techniques are said to purify the internal organs, stimulate the blood, and promote good health. In order to apply the Aikido techniques smoothly and correctly we must be naturally linked to our partner and our environment through *kokyu* at every stage.

6

Kamae: Stance

The stance employed in Aikido is *hanmi*, adapted by the Founder from the classical Yagyu school of swordsmanship. In *hanmi*, the feet are placed triangularly. Keep the spine straight, relax the shoulders, extend the arms naturally in a slight arc, and charge the hands with *ki*. Neither open nor closed, *hanmi* is a stable yet supple posture.

When holding a sword the stance is the same (take caution not to adopt the modern *kendo* stance which is entirely different). Grip the handle tightly with the last two fingers of each hand. Think of the sword as an extension of your body, not a separate instrument. It should point out from the body's center, held neither too high nor too low; the height varies according to the height and stance of your opponent. Swing the sword straight up while inhaling and cut straight down while exhaling.

The Founder demonstrating the correct manner of holding a sword. (When a question arose one day about the proper posture, he posed on the spot in his regular clothes. Photo taken at the Iwama Dojo.)

Side view.

⬅ How to raise the sword.

⬇ How to swing a sword.

When facing an opponent, to avoid being "captured" by his stare, gaze in the direction of his forehead rather than looking at his eyes. When both have the same foot forward, it is called *ai-hanmi*; when each has a different foot advanced, it is called *gyaku-hanmi*. Practitioners often have difficulty estimating the proper *ma-ai* (combative distance); correct *ma-ai* can be gauged in this manner:

Ai-hanmi

Shomen-uchi (direct blow to the head). Initially in *gyaku-hanmi katate-dori* (held by one wrist), both partners withdraw the front leg and step back; this gives the correct *ma-ai*. As soon as *uke* moves forward to deliver *shomen-uchi*, respond with a suitable technique.

Yokomen-uchi (side blow to the head).
Start in *ai-hanmi ryote-dori* (both wrists held);
both partners withdraw the front leg and step
back as in *shomen-uchi*. To escape the force of
the blow, cut deeply to the front while applying *atemi*; grab *uke's* wrist securely to unbalance him, making sure you are out of range
of a follow-up attack.

7

Shiho-nage: Four Directions Throw

Although *shiho-nage* is customarily the first throw to be taught to beginners, it is one technique that all practitioners must continually study and refine. Much more than a device to knock down an opponent, *shiho-nage* contains profound philosophical implications that reveal the heart of Aikido.

The Founder explained *shiho-nage* in terms of *shiho-giri*, "swinging the sword in the four directions." In Aikido, a sword is not for cutting or killing; it is for manifesting the sacredness of life. *Shiho-giri* expresses three principles: gratitude, purification, and realization (*kansha, misogi,* and *kiri-hiraku*).

Shiho-giri is synonymous with *shiho-hai,* "four-direction respect." All of our activities, in and out of the training hall, should begin and end with *rei,* "respect." Respect originates with gratitude, gratitude for all the things responsible for our existence. "Four" symbolizes the Four Gratitudes: gratitude toward the Universal from which we received our animating spirit; gratitude toward our parents from whom we received our body; gratitude toward nature from which we receive our sustenance; and gratitude toward our fellow beings from whom we receive life's daily necessities. We cannot survive without the assistance of others, and must never cease to be grateful in "all directions."

Shiho-giri is *misogi,* the cutting off of the evil that surrounds us and of our own imperfections; the sword purifies us of attachments and defilements, making the heart clear and bright.

Shiho-giri also slashes through all the obstacles that hinder self-realization, thus clearing the path leading to perfection.

Never forget these three principles when performing *shiho-nage.*

Shiho-giri (four-direction cut). Begin in right *hanmi*. Stepping out with the left foot, make the first cut; pivot and make the second cut to the back; step out on the left foot for the third cut; pivot to the right for the fourth cut; then swing the left foot to the front, finishing with one more cut. This is one *shiho-giri* cycle. Repeat the movement leading with the right foot. Follow the regular up-inhale, down-exhale pattern at first, later trying to complete a cycle in one long *kiai*.

Naname kiri-sage kiri-age (diagonal down-stroke, diagonal up-stroke). *Shiho* is not just the four horizontal directions of North, South, East, and West; it must also include the vertical and diagonal, as displayed in this exercise. From right *hanmi*, step out on the left foot, cut down and up, and then diagonally to the rear; cut up diagonally, turn, and cut to the back. Repeat the movement from the right. (The two movements constitute one cycle.) The principle here is that whatever moves down must also move up—there is always a balance of opposites. Breathe as in *shiho-giri*.

Shiho-nage No. 1

Sword-technique. The Founder cautioned us never to concentrate exclusively on facing a single opponent; attacks should be expected from all directions. Here the attack is coming front and back. As soon as the *uke* raise their swords to strike, avoid the path of their blades by stepping to the side with *niho-zenshin zengo-kiri* movement no. 3, i.e., left-right thrust, turn, and cut. Position yourself well to the side of *uke* no. 1.*

*"Uke no. 1" refers to the *uke* initially facing Shirata Sensei.

➡

Body-technique. The movements are exactly the same as in the sword-technique. Step out with the left foot, then the right, turn, and throw *uke* by cutting down. The hips and feet must be solidly planted when executing the throw.

Shiho-nage No. 2

Sword-technique. Slide to the side of *uke* no. 1 and cut; when *uke* no. 2 raises his sword to strike again, swing around with the right leg, cut across his midsection and turn toward *uke* no. 1. ➡

Variation. In this case both *uke* strike from the front. It illustrates the necessity of making as wide a sweep as possible to avoid *uke* no. 2's second cut. ⇨

Body-technique. This is the standard *ura shiho-nage*. Deliver *atemi* to *uke's* face while stepping to his side, grab his wrist, turn, and throw. Note the full sweep of the turning motion; inadequate spin renders the technique ineffective and potentially dangerous for *uke*.

How to apply *atemi* and how to
hold *uke's* wrist in *shiho-nage* no. 2.

Shiho-nage No. 3

Sword-technique.   Slide to the side of *uke* no. 1 and cut; when both *uke* raise their swords to strike again, turn toward *uke* no. 2, step out with the left foot while cutting up, spin, and cut down toward *uke* no. 1. ⇩

⇨

Body-technique. Slide to *uke's* side, take a large step forward with the left foot, turn, and throw.

Shiho-nage No. 4

Sword-technique. Slide to the side of *uke* no. 1 and cut; as both *uke* raise their swords to strike again, step between them with the left foot, cutting up through *uke* no. 1. Turn and cut toward *uke* no. 2.

Body-technique. This is the standard *omote shiho-nage*. As *uke* steps out with his right foot to reach for your left wrist, move forward with your left foot and immediately slide to his side. Advance deeply with the left foot, turn, and throw. Just prior to the throw note Shirata Sensei's classic *shiho-nage* form: hands, head, hips, and feet perfectly aligned.

Front view. Here, instead of cutting down to throw *uke*, bring him to the mat by sinking your hips. This method is recommended when throwing inexperienced practitioners.

Shiho-nage No. 5

Sword-technique. Swing to the inside of *uke* no. 1 and cut; when both *uke* raise their swords to strike again, step out with the left foot, cut up between them, turn, and cut down. ⇩

⇨

Body-technique. No. 5 is a "flowing" (*nagare*) technique. Lead *uke* by sweeping to the rear with the left foot, step in, and throw. Do not break the continuity of the movement.

⇨

⇨

In addition to practicing the five *shiho-nage* forms when held by the wrist as shown above, study their application to *shomen-uchi*, *yokomen-uchi*, thrusts, and other types of attack.

En no irimi on the highest level. Eluding conflict with *uke's yokomen-uchi* attack, Shirata Sensei throws him "free-style" in a seamless flow of *kokyu*—not a trace of stagnation or strain.

8

Irimi-nage:
Entering Throw

In the early days of Aikido, there was no separate group of techniques known as *"irimi-nage."* The concept of *"irimi-nage"* developed slowly, assuming its present forms only after World War II. No other technique is subject to such wide interpretation and execution; in a sense, every practitioner, rightly or wrongly, has his or her own *irimi-nage*. Shirata Sensei distinguishes three kinds of *irimi-nage: en no irimi, sankaku no irimi*, and *chokusen no irimi*.

En no Irimi: Circular Irimi

Although the *irimi*, "entering," technique is derived from Daito-ryu Aiki-jutsu, *en no irimi* is unique to Aikido, the creation of the Founder's last years. *En no irimi* is the one favored by the current Doshu.

In *en no irimi*, one imitates the spinning motion of the earth, drawing the opponent into one's (and by extension, the universe's) sphere to break his posture and throw him in one sweeping movement. Unfortunately, *en no irimi* frequently degenerates into a sort of "act" with the *uke* ungainly propelling and throwing himself down quite independently of the moves of his partner. *En no irimi* must be practiced slowly with full force at first; refrain from trying to throw an opponent without touching him.

Sword-technique. As *uke* comes forward to strike, step to the side and pivot on the left foot, hooking his sword with your own; spin *uke* around, and when he attempts to strike again, step behind him and cut down.

Body-technique. (*Basic technique*). In the same manner as in the sword-technique, cut behind *uke*, securely grabbing his collar and swinging his arm around; glue him to your shoulder, bring the right arm up as shown, and then step in as if cutting down with the sword to throw him. Note especially the extension of the throwing arm, and the angle of the left foot.

Basic technique viewed from the front.

(*Shomen-uchi*). Performed at "normal" speed, Shirata Sensei leaps behind the *uke,* whips him around, guides him up, and knocks him down in a powerful display of *en no irimi*. Direct your attention to Shirata Sensei's remarkable stability as he throws *uke*, and to the unbroken concentration of his *zanshin*.

Sankaku no Irimi: Triangular Entering

Unlike other forms of swordsmanship, there is no direct blade-to-blade confrontation in Aiki-ken; cuts and thrusts are not received, but parried, or better still, avoided entirely. The best way to evade a straight blow is the triangular two-step forward movement (*niho-zenshin*).

Sword-technique. As *uke* comes forward to strike, step out of the line of attack with the left foot, and cut to his rear with the right. Strike at *uke's* "enemy-mind" rather than his physical presence.

Body-technique. (*Ai-hanmi*). Raise up both arms in an arc, step to *uke's* side with the left foot, and then step behind him triangularly with the right foot.

(Gyaku-hanmi). The grip is reversed, but the movements remain the same—one step, two steps, and down.

Chokusen no Irimi: Direct Entering

Chokusen no irimi is best described in one of the Founder's "Songs of the Way" (*doka*):

> Seeing me before him,
> The enemy attacks,
> But in a flash,
> I am already
> Behind him.

⇨

Sword-technique. As *uke* comes forward to strike, step out and immediately pivot on the left foot, swinging the right leg around; withdraw the left leg and cut deeply to the rear.

Body-technique. (*Ai-hanmi*). Step to *uke's* right, grasp his collar, and move directly behind him by pivoting on the left foot; cut down across his forehead with the right hand while withdrawing the right foot.

(*Tsuki*). After evading *uke's* thrust, pivot on the left foot; hold *uke's* sleeve and place your hand across his forehead while stepping back to bring him down.

Graphic illustration of the
Founder's *doka*.
This page:
Shomen-uchi;

Next page:
Tachi-dori.

9

Kaiten:
Open and Turn

The third pillar of Aikido is *kaiten*, "open and turn" techniques. If *shiho* is a symbol of gratitude, and *en no irimi* a symbol of harmony, *kaiten* is a symbol of openness and flexibility. *Kaiten* permits us to turn around any attack, thus clearing the way for true spiritual progress. Whatever arises must be approached with all three pillars—one or two will be insufficient.

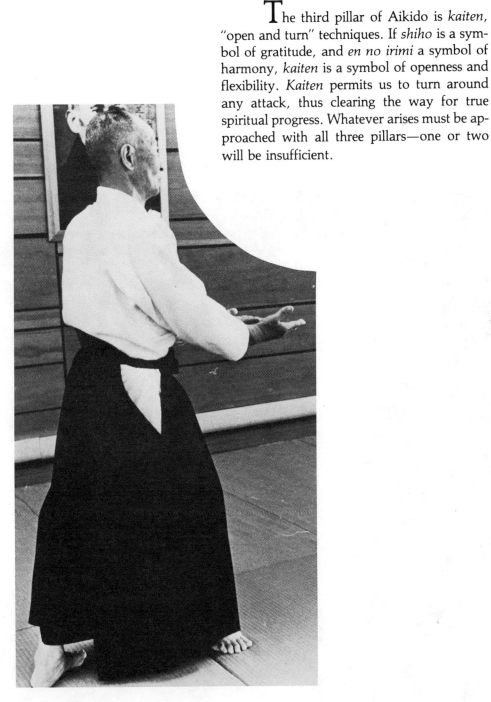

The *kaiten* stance.

The Founder demonstrating *tai-no-tenkan,* "body-turn."

Kaiten No. 1

Basic movement. (1) Pivot on the right foot and perform *tai no tenkan*, "body turn." Keep the wrists at approximately the same level during the turn, and be careful not to look down or twist the head to the side. The right foot should angle out for stability when the turn is completed. Do not lean forward. (2) Withdraw the right leg and assume a *hanmi* stance.

Body-technique. (*Sokumen irimi-nage*). Perform *tai no tenkan,* aligning yourself with *uke*; hold his wrist from the bottom and disengage your hand. Lift up both arms while stepping back with the right foot and throw.

(*Kote-gaeshi-nage*). *Kaiten* no. 1 is the basis of *kote-gaeshi*, "wrist turn-out" throws.

A. (*Katate-dori*). Perform *tai no tenkan*, neutralizing *uke's* power; grab his wrist with both hands as shown, step back, and throw him with a strong twist of the hips. ⇨

B. (*Shomen-uchi*). Turn behind *uke's* blow, and firmly apply the *kote-gaeshi* grip (note Shirata Sensei's "open" stance); step back, plant your feet solidly on the mat, twist your hips forcefully, and throw.

The *kaiten kote-gaeshi* movement is especially effective when countering a knife attack.

C. (*Suwari yokomen-uchi*). First "open" to the front to escape the force of *uke's* blow; push up his arm from underneath with your left hand, and "open" to his side. Apply *kote-gaeshi*, withdraw the right knee, and throw.

Kaiten No. 2 ➡

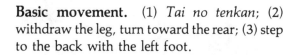

Basic movement. (1) *Tai no tenkan*; (2) withdraw the leg, turn toward the rear; (3) step to the back with the left foot.

Body-technique. *(Juji-nage). Tai no tenkan* is the first movement; the second is to withdraw the left leg and turn in while shooting *atemi* to *uke's* head; as *uke* blocks the *atemi* with his left hand, grasp his wrist with your hand while maintaining your hold on his right wrist. Cross *uke's* arms at the elbow joints (keep your left arm straight and pointed down); step in and throw with movement number three. (Release your grip so *uke* can take *ukemi*.)

(*Ikkyo-nage*). The movements are the same except that you let go of *uke's* left wrist and push his elbow to throw him. ⇨

Variations (not illustrated). Take hold of both wrists, but do not cross them and throw by stepping in; pin instead of throw *uke* with *ikkyo*; on movement number three step in and apply *sankyo* (throw or pin). May also be used against *shomen-uchi, tsuki,* etc.

(*Jo-dori*). Perform *tai no tenkan* and grip the *jo*; step back and turn in, then step forward and throw straight out. Note how the grip is shifted during movement number two.

Kaiten No. 3

Basic movement. (1) *Tai no tenkan;* (2) withdraw the right leg and turn; (3) step out with the left foot; (4) turn. ⬇

Body-technique. Perform *tai no tenkan;* on movement number two grip both of *uke's* wrists, then step in with the left foot, immediately turn, and throw. ➡

Kaiten-nage

(*Uchi-mawari*). Completely open *uke's* posture by stepping to the side and delivering *atemi* to his face (Shirata Sensei holds on to *uke's* blocking hand to preclude a counterattack); cut deeply to *uke's* rear while entering on the left foot and turning; push his head down, grab his wrist, step in, and throw, projecting him away from your body.

(*Soto-mawari*). In this case turn to *uke's* side; withdraw the right leg circularly, bind *uke's* arm with your elbow, spin, and throw.

10

Kokyu-ho Waza: Breath-Power Techniques

Breath-power techniques are not a means to throw or pin an opponent; they are used to develop *kokyu-ryoku*. It is not possible to acquire breath-power through free-form, flowing techniques alone, so do not execute *kokyu-ho* techniques in a hurried manner. Allow *uke* to firmly take hold of your arm or wrists and perform the exercises with full extension.

Standing Kokyu-ho Waza No. 1

After *uke* grips your arm tightly with both his hands (*morote-dori*), exhale and step in front of him; inhale while raising your arms, move forward on the left foot, turn and grip *uke's* elbow and wrist; exhale while you either pin or throw him.

Standing Kokyu-ho Waza No. 2 (throwing technique)

This time after advancing the two steps, move under *uke's* arms with the right foot and finish with either a pin or throw. Same breath sequence as in no. 2.

(pinning technique)

Standing Kokyu-ho Waza No. 3

Exhale when *uke* grabs your arm; pivot on the right foot and inhale while raising the arms (note how *uke's* posture is broken); exhale while withdrawing your right leg (hold his elbow), and throw.

Standing Kokyu-ho Waza No. 4

Exhale when your arm is held; inhale while slanting the left leg toward *uke* and fully extending the grasped arm; exhale as you step behind him and throw.

Sitting Kokyu-ho Waza No. 1

As soon as your wrists are held, perform the basic sitting *kokyu-undo* movement; *uke* will be raised straight up as you inhale. Exhale as you throw him to the front and pin him with *tegatana*. ⇨

Sitting Kokyu-ho Waza No. 2

The same as no. 1, but throw *uke* to the rear.
⇩

Sitting Kokyu-ho Waza No. 3

Break *uke's* hold by crossing your hands and sliding to his side (inhale); grip his wrist and sleeve as shown, and throw him to the front (exhale). This is the *gedan* (hands at the lower level) exercise; also practice its *jodan* (hands at the upper level) form. ➡

Sitting Kokyu-ho Waza No. 4

This is the *tenchi* (heaven and earth) variation; inhale while lifting the right hand toward the sky and dropping the left hand toward the ground; exhale while moving forward with the right knee and throw. ⇩

11

Taninsu-gake: Multiple Attack

As mentioned previously, every Aikido technique presupposes multiple attack and the movements remain essentially the same regardless of the number of opponents. To increase one's breath-power Shirata Sensei recommends practicing the *kokyu* techniques while being held from both sides.

Example No. 1

This is the applied form of standing *kokyu-undo*. Exhale when first held; withdraw the left foot, bring the elbows tightly against the sides of your body, and then inhale while raising the arms and stepping forward with the left foot. Step forward with the right foot while exhaling and throw the *uke* by lowering yourself all the way to the mat.

Example No. 2

Standing in right *hanmi*, exhale while withdrawing the right foot; inhale while bringing up your arms in a large circle directly over *ukes'* heads. Exhale while stepping forward on the left foot and throw.

Example No. 3

Exhale while sliding toward *uke* no. 1; withdraw the left foot while inhaling and raising your arms. Exhale as you step back and throw *uke* no 1; inhale as you move toward *uke* no. 2, step forward with the right leg, and throw him with *ikkyo-nage* (exhale).

Example No. 4

Exhale when held. While inhaling slide to the side of *uke* no. 1 by withdrawing the left leg; the right arm is extended toward uke no. 1, and the left hand is brought up from under *uke* no. 2's arms. Step behind *uke* no. 2 with the left foot, and throw (exhale).

Turn toward *uke* no. 1 (inhale), step forward with the right foot, and throw (exhale) as in the previous example.

Example No. 5

As the two *uke* move in to deliver *shomen-uchi*, step between them with the left foot, pivot to the inside, and apply *kote-gaeshi*; step back with the right foot and throw *uke* simultaneously.

Example No. 6

Step out with the right foot while raising the right arm and pulling your left arm toward *uke* no. 1 (inhale); after crossing all three *uke's* arms grab *uke* no. 1's wrist and elbow and push them down (exhale). (Incidently, the sum total age of the three six-footers holding on to Shirata Sensei does not add up to his seventy years.)

Example No. 7

Step behind *uke* no. 1 and *uke* no. 2 while pulling *uke* no. 3's arm up from underneath (exhale); lift up and cross all of their arms (inhale). Step forward on the right foot and push them down (exhale).

12

Osae Waza:
Pinning Techniques

Aikido pinning techniques are not for the purpose of inflicting pain; they are exercises designed to stretch and strengthen the joints. When one is a new practitioner on the receiving end, these techniques are indeed punishing, but through constant training the stiff joints gradually become so flexible that they no longer hurt at all. The Founder told his disciples that once the techniques stop causing pain it means that the joints are cleansed of "impurities." (Shirata Sensei recalls that since the Founder's techniques never lost their effectiveness, no student could claim that his joints were totally free of "dust.")

With the exception of the basic *suwari ikkyo* pin, all the techniques illustrated here are complex variants.

Dai ikkyo

Suwari shomen-uchi ikkyo. This and *katate-dori shiho-nage* are the most fundamental Aikido techniques. When Shirata Sensei was admitted as the Founder's student he was allowed to practice only these two techniques for months. It is advisable to think of *ikkyo,* and the other pins as well, in terms of the inhale-exhale pattern; inhale when rising to counter *uke's* attack, and exhale when applying the pin.

(*Omote*). As soon as *uke* raises his arm to strike, securely grab his wrist and elbow, advance on the left knee, and then step out with the right leg. Keep *uke's* wrist glued to your thigh and slide his arm down to the mat for the pin. Stand on the toes during the pin, extend the arms in a slight arc, and do not lean over—the spine should be straight. ⇨

(*Ura*). Swing around in one big sweep, making sure the arm holding *uke's* elbow is fully extended. Pin as above—always at the elbow, never at the shoulder. ➡

Dai-nikyo

Suwari kata-dori nikyo. (*Omote*). Shoot *atemi* to *uke's* face while unbalancing him to the side; securely grasp his wrist and elbow and then advance on the right knee. Step out with the left foot and apply *nikyo* as shown, directing *uke's* little finger toward his center and twisting his elbow toward your side. Finish with the standard *nikyo* pin.

(*Ura*). Apply *nikyo* as shown; slide toward *uke* and knock him back to the mat with your right hand. Apply *nikyo* once more.

Dai-sankyo

Yokomen-uchi sankyo. (*Omote*). After receiving *yokomen-uchi* (not shown), cut in and grasp *uke's* wrist while delivering *atemi* to his face; lift his arm by bringing up your right hand under his wrist. Step in with the left foot and apply *ikkyo* to break his posture. Advance deeply on the right foot and bring him down to the mat. Shift the grip, i.e., take his right hand with your left, and hold his elbow with your right hand. Pull his arm to the front and pin him from the outside as shown.

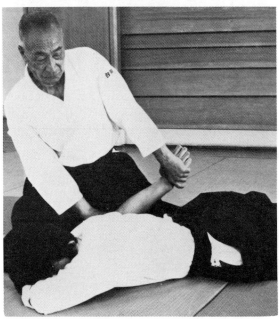

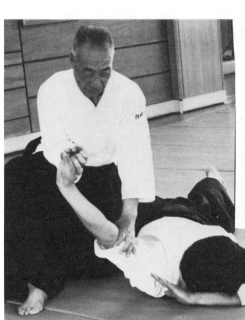

How to shift the grip.

(*Ura*). Neutralize the blow as shown. After raising *uke's* arm, align yourself with his side. Apply *sankyo*; then step back with the right foot while directing *uke's* arm upward, causing him to "float." Bring him down to the mat by withdrawing the right foot and pressing down hard on his elbow.

To pin him, first grab his elbow with your left hand, bring his wrist toward you, and then hold it tightly with your right hand; take hold of his left arm with your left hand and place it next to his other arm. (This is an arrest technique for subduing and binding a suspect.)

(*Jo-dori*). After performing *tai no tenkan* to evade *uke's* thrust, grasp the *jo* with your left hand while shooting *atemi* with your right hand to *uke's* face; as soon as he attempts to block the *atemi* grasp his wrist and step in with the *kaiten nage* movement, apply *sankyo*, and pin as shown.

(*Tachi-dori*). Step out of the line of *uke's* attack and deliver *atemi* to his face; move forward, turn, apply *sankyo*, and pin.

Dai-yonkyo

Yokomen-uchi yonkyo-nage. (*Omote*). Cut in and take hold of *uke's* wrist with both hands; apply *yonkyo,* driving up *uke's* arm and causing him to turn. Step in front of him with your left foot, turn, and take hold of his elbow; flip *uke* down by stepping in with the right foot. Spin him around and apply the *yonkyo* pin as shown.

⇨

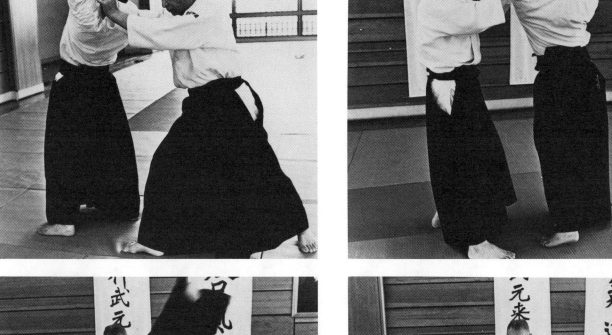

Tsuki yonkyo-nage. (*Ura*). Cut inside *uke's* thrust and grasp his wrist with both hands; apply *yonkyo* from the *top* of *uke's* arm. Lift up his arm, step forward on the right foot, and throw.

Viewed from the side.

Dai-gokyo

Yokomen-uchi gokyo. Deal with *uke's yokomen* blow in the customary fashion; after raising up his arm, grab his elbow from above, turn, and bring him down to the mat. Pin *uke* by kneeling on his left arm with your left leg, picking up his right arm with your right hand, grabbing his wrist, and stretching his arm straight back.

13

Ushiro Waza:
Rear Techniques

"Even when facing only one opponent, act as if another is behind you." The Founder considered *ushiro-waza*, especially *ushiro eri-dori* (rear collar hold), to be extremely valuable since they heighten one's intuition. One must learn to respond to an unseen attack. Four basic movements are involved in rear techniques.

Rear Technique No. 1

Sword-technique. As the *uke* raise their swords to strike, slide to the side out of the line of attack, positioning your sword so that you can deflect either blow, and then cut down diagonally toward *uke* no. 2 as you withdraw the right leg. When they attack again, step between them on the right foot and cut toward *uke* no. 1.

Body-technique. Withdraw the right leg, grasp *uke's* wrist tightly, step in with the right foot, and throw *uke* no. 2 toward *uke* no. 1. Immediately move to counter *uke* no. 1's attack, in this case by *kokyu-nage*.

Viewed from the front.

Rear Technique No. 2

Sword-technique. Slide out and step back with the left foot; step between the two *uke* on the second attack and cut down.

Body-technique. Slide´ to the right and deliver *atemi* (or block his *atemi*, depending on the case) to *uke* no. 2; withdraw the left leg, grab *uke* no. 2's wrist and step forward to throw him with *ikkyo-nage.* Deal with *uke* no. 1's second attack in an appropriate manner.

Rear Technique No. 3

Sword-technique. Step diagonally to the right with the left foot, withdraw the right foot and cut toward *uke* no. 2; as they strike again, turn toward *uke* no. 1, step in with the left foot, cut up, turn, and cut down. ⇨

Body-technique. Spin around with the left foot, then the right, binding *uke* no. 2's arm and throwing him with a sharp turn of the hips; step forward to greet *uke* no. 1. ⬇

Viewed from the front.

Rear Technique No. 4

Sword-technique. Step out with the left foot, then the right; swing in with the left leg and cut diagonally at *uke* no. 2. As they strike again, move out on the left leg between them and cut down. ➪

191

Body-technique. Step out of the line of *uke* no. 1's attack with the left foot, swing the right leg around, grab *uke* no. 2's sleeve as shown, apply *atemi* to the side of his head, and throw; rise and take on *uke* no. 1. ⇩

How to throw *uke* no. 2.

Glossary of
Japanese Terms

ai 合 (harmony, coming together, unification) *Ai* is the active principle of *ai-ki-do*.

ai 愛 (love) The spirit of love is the spirit of harmony. Not selfish, limited affection for a particular person or group, but all-embracing, compassionate love for all things.

ai-hanmi 合半身 (mutual stance) When both partners have the same foot advanced, it is known as *ai-hanmi*.

aiki 合気 (blending of *ki*) All elements of the universe arise through the blending of positive and negative *ki*; practitioners of Aikido attempt to harmonize their *ki* with both that of their partner and that of the larger environment.

Aikido 合気道 (The Way of Harmony) After decades of severe physical and spiritual forging, the Founder chose this name to represent his unique system.

Aiki Jinja 合気神社 (Aiki Shrine) The Founder's spirit is enshrined in this building, located in Iwama, Ibaragi Prefecture.

aiki-ken 合気剣 (*aiki* sword techniques) Swordsmanship according to the principles of Aikido.

Aiki Okami 合気大神 (The Great Spirit of Aiki) The supreme symbol of those ideals the Founder esteemed most highly.

atemi 当身 (strike) The defensive blow used to neutralize the *ki* of your partner, i.e., put him or her off balance so a technique can be effectively applied. It is not meant to inflict injury.

Bu 武 (martial ardor) In Aikido, *Bu* signifies valor and indomitable spirit, not contention and strife. Aikido is the ultimate expression of *Bu*, which originally meant to prevent two weapons from coming together.

budo 武道 (martial ways) "Ways" originating in the martial arts, e.g., Judo from *jujutsu*.

budoka 武道家 (martial way practitioner)

chinkon-kishin 鎮魂帰神 (calming the spirit and returning to the divine) A special meditation technique practiced by Omoto-kyo believers.

chi no kokyu 地の呼吸 (the breath of earth) The second stage of breath-meditation.

chokusen no irimi 直線の入身 (direct entry) The irimi technique in which one enters directly behind one's partner.

Daito-ryu 大東流 A traditional system of Aiki-jutsu.

do 道 (Way) In Japan, any art that is practiced to develop both technical and spiritual maturity is considered a *do*, a "Way" to harmonize body and mind.

dojo 道場 (training hall) The name applied to Buddhist temples and any training hall where a Way is practiced.

doka 道歌 (songs of the Way) *Waka*, 5-7-5-7-7 syllable poems, with a spiritual message. The Founder composed many *doka* that present the essence of Aikido.

Doshu 道主 (Grandmaster) Following the traditional Japanese custom, the position of Doshu has been made hereditary. The current Doshu, Ueshiba Kisshomaru, is the Founder's son.

en no irimi 円の入身 (circular entry) The irimi technique in which one enters one's partner circularly.

fudo no shisei 不動の姿勢 (immovable posture) Sitting or standing, one must always be in an immovable posture, not rigid but unperturbable.

gedan 下段 (lower level) Sword (or hands) held at a lower level.

gokyo 五教 (number five pinning technique)

gyaku-hanmi 逆半身 (reverse stance) When both partners have opposite feet advanced, it is known as *gyaku-hanmi*.

hanmi 半身 (half open stance) The basic Aikido stance with the feet placed triangularly.

hito 人 (human being) "A human being is the child of the Divine, a living shrine of the most holy," was a favorite saying of the Founder.

Hombu Dojo 本部道場 (Headquarters Training Hall) Located in a modern three-story building on the site of the original *Kobukan Dojo* in the Shinjuku ward of Tokyo, the *Hombu Dojo* is headquarters of both the Japanese and international Aikido associations.

iki 息 (breath) *Iki* refers more to the physical act of respiration, while *kokyu* signifies the deeper cosmological aspects of breathing.

ikkyo 一教 (number one pinning technique)

irimi nage 入身投 (entering throw) The second of the three pillars of Aikido throwing techniques.

jin no kokyu 人の呼吸 (the breath of human beings) The third stage of breath-meditation.

jodan 上段 (upper level) Sword (or hands) held at an upper level.

jo-dori 杖取 (jo taking) Techniques for disarming an opponent armed with a *jo*.

juji-nage 十字投 (crossed arms throw) A throw executed when one's partner's arms are crossed at right angles.

kaiden 皆伝 (master's certificate) The final license awarded according to the classical martial art teaching system.

kaiso 開祖 (Founder) Ueshiba Morihei is commonly referred to by either this term or by *O-sensei*, "Great-teacher."

kaiten 開転 (open and turn) The third pillar of Aikido throwing techniques.

kamae 構え (stance) This is the "combative" stance assumed when facing an opponent.

kami 神 (deity, divine spirit, holy inspiration, guardian angel, exalted human being) The Japanese conception of *kami* has no direct parallel in Western religious terminology. *Kami-sama* was the Founder's expression for the Ultimate Principle of the universe.

kansha 感謝 (gratitude) Aikido places great emphasis on the expression of gratitude, not just to our instructors and fellow practitioners, but to all members of society and all elements of creation.

kata 型 (fixed form) Predetermined sequences in set forms. Used in the martial arts as a learning technique.

katate-dori 片手取 (held by one hand)

kenjutsu 剣術 (sword techniques) Aikido techniques performed while holding a sword.

ki 気 (vital energy) *Ki,* the life-stuff of the universe, has no English equivalent. An essential element of all aspects of oriental culture—philosophy, medicine, art, physical training—the full significance of *ki* only becomes clear through firsthand experience.

kiai 気合 (full of *ki*) On the physical plane, *kiai* is manifest as a piercing shout emanating from the depths of one's being; on the spiritual plane, it is manifest as a steady outpouring of vital energy.

kikai tanden 気海丹田 (ocean field of *ki*) In the Orient, one's physical and spiritual center is thought to be located about two inches beneath one's navel in the *kikai tanden*. As the source of physical strength and mental power, it must be nourished through *kokyu* and *ki* development exercises.

kimusubi 気産 (linking *ki*) To be linked to the *ki* of another person or thing is to be in *kimusubi*, a fertile state that fosters new life. When the *ki* of a man and the *ki* of a woman comes together in *kimusubi,* a new being is created.

kirihiraku 切り開く (cut and open) The movements of the *aiki* sword cut off defilements and open a path for spiritual progress.

kirikami 切り紙 (first certificate) The initial license

granted according to the classical martial art teaching system.

Kobukan 皇武館 The name of the Founder's original training hall in Tokyo.

kokyu 呼吸 (animating breath) The concept of *kokyu* is similar to that of the Hindu idea of *prana*, "life breath of the cosmos." When one's *kokyu* is full and deep, one is in tune with the workings of the universe.

kokyu-ho 呼吸法 (breath-meditation) A special set of meditation and development techniques aimed at calming the spirit and establishing true *kokyu*.

kokyu-roku 呼吸力 (breath-power) The irresistible power that emanates from true *kokyu*.

kokyu-undo 呼吸運動 (breath movement) Techniques used to develop *kokyu-roku*. They are performed sitting (*suwari*) and standing (*tate*), either individually or with a partner.

kote-gaeshi 小手返 (wrist turn-out throw)

kotodama 言霊 (sacred words) The ancient Shinto science of sacred sound and speech.

ma-ai 間合 (combative distance) The proper interval between two partners; it varies according to the height of the practitioners and whether or not they are holding weapons.

makoto no kokyu 誠の呼吸 (true breath) Another name for breath-meditation.

masakatsu akatsu 正勝吾勝 (By acting in accordance with the truth we always emerge victorious) A favorite saying of the Founder that sums up the ethics of Aikido.

menkyo 免許 (teacher's certificate) The third license granted according to the classical martial art teaching system.

misogi 禊 (purification) Various defilements obscure our essentially pure and godlike nature; through *misogi*, purification of body and mind, we can remove such impurities and restore our true image. Although *misogi* rites usually involve water purification (e.g., in a waterfall), the Founder considered all of the Aikido techniques to be forms of *misogi*.

mokuroku 目録 (catalog of techniques) The second license granted according to the classical martial art teaching system.

morote-dori 諸手取 (held by two hands)

nagare 流 (flow) The unbroken projection of *ki* during the execution of a technique.

niho zenshin zengo kiri 二歩前進前後切り (two steps forward, turn and cut) A basic movement of aikido swordmanship.

nikkyo 二教 (number two pinning technique)

ninja • ninjutsu 忍者 • 忍術 Ninja were special espionage agents employed by samurai lords. The efficacy of *ninja* combat and avoidance

techniques has been greatly exaggerated in popular fiction and folklore.

omote-ura 表 裏 (forward, backward) To facilitate memorization of the basic movements, most Aikido techniques are divided into *omote*, "moving forward," and *ura* "moving behind." Actually, the full range of techniques encompasses many other movements beyond just *omote* and *ura*.

Omoto-kyo 大本教 (The Teaching of the Great Origin) The religion established early in the twentieth century by Deguchi Nao and Deguchi Onisaburo. The Founder was a fervent believer in Omoto-kyo from the time of his late thirties.

O-sensei 大先生 (Great Teacher) A common way of referring to Ueshiba Morihei.

Oshiki-uchi (*o-dome*) 御式内 （ 御留め ） The techniques of Daito-ryu Aiki-jutsu.

rei 礼 (bow) The formal gesture of respect and gratitude used by Aikido practitioners.

ryote-dori 両手取 (both hands held)

sankaku no irimi 三角の入身 (triangular entry) One enters to the side and then to the rear of one's partner in a triangular pattern.

sankyo 三教 (number three pinning technique)

sashin-yutai 左進右退 (advance with the left, withdraw with the right) Standard footwork in Aikido.

seiki 生気 (vital force) The vital force that enlivens the universe.

seimei 生命 (life) When we are endowed with *ki* and *kokyu* we possess *seimei*, "life."

seiza 正座・静座 (correct sitting, calm sitting) The classic martial art sitting posture.

sensei 先生 (teacher) A title used for one's instructor.

shiai 試合 (contest) Competition is contrary to the spirit of Aikido; if contests were allowed they would be *shiai*, 死合 "death matches," since the techniques, if applied recklessly, can be fatal.

shihan 師範 (master instructor) A title used for the highest ranking teachers.

shiho-giri 四方切り (four-directions cut) The basic Aikido sword movement.

shiho-hai 四方拝 (four-directions respect) Originally a Shinto rite employed by the Japanese emperor to express his gratitude to the deities in all directions, the Founder interpreted *shiho-giri* as *shiho-hai*, "four-directions respect." That is, each cut symbolizes our respect and gratitude for (1) the Universal, (2) our parents, (3) nature, and (4) fellow beings.

shiho-nage 四方投 (four-directions throw) The first pillar of Aikido throwing techniques.

shikko 膝行 (knee walking)

Shin Bu honrai fuji 神武本来不二 (the Way of the Gods and the Way of Bu are originally not two different paths). A saying of Sensei's that expresses the essential unity of shinto and Budo.

shinken shobu 真剣勝負 (fight to the death) Literally, *shinken shobu* is a fight with a live sword; figuratively, it means to throw oneself single-mindedly into one's practice.

shomen-uchi 正面打 (direct blow to the head)

Shuren Dojo 修錬道場 The name of the dojo founded by O-sensei in Iwama, Ibaragi Prefecture.

soto-mawari 外廻り (turning out) Movement to the side of one's partner.

tachi-dori 太刀取 (sword taking) Techniques used to disarm an opponent armed with a sword.

tai-jutsu 体術 (body techniques) Techniques performed without weapons.

tai no tenkan 体の転開 (body turn)

tai-sabaki 体捌き (body movement) Body movement in Aikido should be free-flowing, natural, and prudent.

take 武 (martial ardor) An alternative pronunciation of the Chinese character *Bu*.

Takemusu Aiki 武産合気 (Inexhaustible Fount of Aiki) The Founder's term for the unlimited creativity of Aikido.

taninsu-gake 多人数掛 (multiple attack) Even when practicing with a single partner, one should always assume simultaneous attacks from all directions. In *taninsu-gake* one deals with two or more opponents.

tegatana 手刀 (hand sword) Since Aikido techniques are based on sword movements, the hand, with the fingers spread actively projecting *ki*, should function as a sword.

tenchi 天地 (heaven and earth) A common expression in Aikido; one should think of oneself as a miniature universe, rooted to the earth while reaching toward heaven. There is also a whole range of techniques called *tenchi-nage*, "heaven and earth throw."

ten no kokyu 天の呼吸 (the breath of heaven) The first stage of breath-meditation.

uchi-deshi 内弟子 (inner disciple) A disciple who lives in the *dojo* and act as a twenty-four hour trainee/attendant to a master.

uchi-mawari 内廻り (turn-in) To step inside one's partner's arm.

Ueshiba Juku 植芝塾 The name of the Founder's first *dojo*; it was located on the grounds of the Omoto-kyo compound in Ayabe.

uke 受 (receiver) The partner who "receives" the technique.

ukemi 受身 (fall) The act of taking a controlled fall when thrown.

ushiro-waza 後技 (rear techniques) Techniques applied when one is attacked from the rear.

yokomen-uchi 横面打 (side blow to the head)

yonkyo 四教 (number four pinning technique)

zanshin 残心 (unbroken concentration) *Zanshin* is the "follow through" of a technique; one is connected to one's partner even after the throw in an unbroken flow of *ki*, simultaneously ready to receive any new attack. Shirata Sensei's *zanshin* is particularly effective.

front cover:
Shirata Rinjiro demonstrating Aiki swordsmanship before a huge portrait of Ueshiba Morihei, founder of Aikido. To the right is the calligraphy of Aiki Okami, "The Great Spirit of Aiki."